Kaplan Publishing are constantly fi' ''
ways to make a difference to your s
exciting online resources really do (
different to students looking for exa

GW01091522

This book comes with free MyKaplan online resources so that you can study anytime, anywhere. This free online resource is not sold separately and is included in the price of the book.

Having purchased this book, you have access to the following online study materials:

CONTENT	ACCA (including FFA,FAB,FMA)		FIA (excluding FFA,FAB,FMA)	
	Text	Kit	Text	Kit
Electronic version of the book	✓	✓	✓	✓
Check Your Understanding Test with instant answers	✓			
Material updates	✓	✓	✓	✓
Latest official ACCA exam questions*		✓		
Extra question assistance using the signpost icon**		✓		
Timed questions with an online tutor debrief using clock icon***		✓		
Interim assessment including questions and answers	✓		✓	
Technical answers	✓	✓	✓	✓

*   Excludes F1, F2, F3, F4, FAB, FMA and FFA; for all other papers includes a selection of questions, as released by ACCA

**   For ACCA P1-P7 only

*** Excludes F1, F2, F3, F4, FAB, FMA and FFA

How to access your online resources

Kaplan Financial students will already have a MyKaplan account and these extra resources will be available to you online. You do not need to register again, as this process was completed when you enrolled. If you are having problems accessing online materials, please ask your course administrator.

If you are not studying with Kaplan and did not purchase your book via a Kaplan website, to unlock your extra online resources please go to www.mykaplan.co.uk/addabook (even if you have set up an account and registered books previously). You will then need to enter the ISBN number (on the title page and back cover) and the unique pass key number contained in the scratch panel below to gain access.

You will also be required to enter additional information during this process to set up or confirm your account details.

If you purchased through Kaplan Flexible Learning or via the Kaplan Publishing website you will automatically receive an e-mail invitation to MyKaplan. Please register your details using this email to gain access to your content. If you do not receive the e-mail or book content, please contact Kaplan Publishing.

Your Code and Information

This code can only be used once for the registration of one book online. This registration and your online content will expire when the final sittings for the examinations covered by this book have taken place. Please allow one hour from the time you submit your book details for us to process your request.

Please scratch the film to access your MyKaplan code.

Please be aware that this code is case-sensitive and you will need to include the dashes within the passcode, but not when entering the ISBN. For further technical support, please visit www.MyKaplan.co.uk

KAPLAN PUBLISHING

ACCA Diploma in Financial and
Management Accounting (RQF Level 2)

MA1

Management Information

STUDY TEXT

British Library Cataloguing-in-Publication Data

A catalogue record for this book is available from the British Library.

Published by:

Kaplan Publishing UK
Unit 2 The Business Centre
Molly Millars Lane
Wokingham
RG41 2QZ

ISBN: 978-1-78740-382-6

© Kaplan Financial Limited, 2019

Printed and bound in Great Britain.

Acknowledgments

We are grateful to the Association of Chartered Certified Accountants for permission to reproduce past examination questions. The answers have been prepared by Kaplan Publishing.

All rights reserved. No part of this publication may be reproduced, stored in a retrieval system, or transmitted, in any form or by any means, electronic, mechanical, photocopying, recording or otherwise, without the prior written permission of Kaplan Publishing.

The text in this material and any others made available by any Kaplan Group company does not amount to advice on a particular matter and should not be taken as such. No reliance should be placed on the content as the basis for any investment or other decision or in connection with any advice given to third parties. Please consult your appropriate professional adviser as necessary. Kaplan Publishing Limited and all other Kaplan group companies expressly disclaim all liability to any person in respect of any losses or other claims, whether direct, indirect, incidental, consequential or otherwise arising in relation to the use of such materials.

These materials are reviewed by the ACCA examining team. The objective of the review is to ensure that the material properly covers the syllabus and study guide outcomes, used by the examining team in setting the exams, in the appropriate breadth and depth. The review does not ensure that every eventuality, combination or application of examinable topics is addressed by the ACCA Approved Content. Nor does the review comprise a detailed technical check of the content as the Approved Content Provider has its own quality assurance processes in place in this respect.

CONTENTS

Quality and accuracy are of the utmost importance to us so if you spot an error in any of our products, please send an email to mykaplanreporting@kaplan.com with full details.

Our Quality Co-ordinator will work with our technical team to verify the error and take action to ensure it is corrected in future editions.

INTRODUCTION

This is the new edition of the FIA study text for MA1 *Management Information,* approved by the ACCA and fully updated and revised according to the examiner's comments.

Tailored to fully cover the syllabus, this Study Text has been written specifically for FIA students. Clear and comprehensive style, numerous examples and highlighted key terms help you to acquire the information easily. Plenty of activities and self-test questions enable you to practise what you have learnt.

At the end of most of the chapters you will find multiple-choice questions. These are exam-style questions and will give you a very good idea of the way you will be tested in your examination.

ACCA SUPPORT

For additional support with your studies please also refer to the ACCA Global website.

SYLLABUS AND STUDY GUIDE

Position of the subject in the overall syllabus

No prior knowledge is required before commencing study for MA1. This subject provides the basic techniques required to use a computer system safely and to effectively recognise, provide and maintain management information.

Candidates require a sound understanding of the methods and techniques covered in this subject to enable them to move on to the more complex systems and management control problems covered at subsequent levels.

Some of the methods introduced in this subject are revisited and extended in MA2, *Managing Costs and Finances.*

Syllabus

A   THE NATURE AND PURPOSE OF COST AND MANAGEMENT ACCOUNTING

1   Nature of business organisation and accounting systems

2   Nature and purpose of management information

B   SOURCE DOCUMENTS AND CODING

1   Sources of information

2   Coding system

C   COST CLASSIFICATION AND MEASUREMENT

1   Cost classification and behaviour

2   Cost units, cost centres, profit centres and investment centres

D   RECORDING COSTS

1   Accounting for materials

2   Accounting for labour

3   Accounting for other expenses

4   Accounting for product costs

E   THE SPREADSHEET SYSTEM

1   Spreadsheets overview

2   Creating and using spreadsheets

3   Presenting and printing spreadsheet data/information

Key areas of the syllabus

All areas of the syllabus are equally important.

STUDY GUIDE

A THE NATURE AND PURPOSE OF COST AND MANAGEMENT ACCOUNTING

1 Nature of business organisation and accounting systems   Ch. 1

(a) Describe the organisation, and main functions, of an office as a centre for information and administration.

(b) Describe the function and use of a manual of policies, procedures and best practices.

(c) Identify the main types of transactions undertaken by a business and the key personnel involved in initiating, processing and completing transactions.

(d) Explain the need for effective control over transactions.

(e) Explain and illustrate the principles and practice of double-entry book-keeping.

(f) Describe and illustrate the use of ledgers and prime entry records in both integrated and interlocking accounting systems.

(g) Identify the key features, functions and benefits of a computerised accounting system.

2 Management information   Ch. 2

(a) State the purpose of management information.

(b) Compare cost and management accounting with external financial reporting.

(c) Distinguish between data and information.

(d) Describe the features of useful management information.

(e) Describe and identify sources and categories of information.

(f) Explain the limitations of cost and management accounting information.

(g) Describe the role of a trainee accountant in a cost and management accounting system.

B SOURCE DOCUMENTS AND CODING

1 Source documents   Ch's 4–7

(a) Describe the material control cycle (including the concept of 'free' inventory, but excluding control levels and EOQ) and the documentation necessary to order, receive, store and issue materials.

(b) Describe the procedures and documentation to ensure the correct authorisation, analysis and recording of direct and indirect material costs.

(c) Describe the procedures and documentation to ensure the correct authorisation, coding, analysis and recording of direct and indirect labour and expenses.

(d) Describe the procedures and documentation to ensure the correct analysis and recording of sales.

2 Coding system   Ch. 4

(a) Explain and illustrate the use of codes in categorising and processing transactions.

(b) Explain and illustrate different methods of coding data. (including sequential, hierarchical, block, faceted and mnemonic)

(c) Identify and correct errors in coding of revenue and expenses.

C COST CLASSIFICATION AND MEASUREMENT

1 Cost classification   Ch. 3- 8

(a) Explain cost classification and describe the variety of cost classifications used for different purposes in a cost accounting system, including by responsibility, function, behaviour, direct/indirect.

(b) Describe and illustrate the nature of variable, fixed and mixed (semi-variable, stepped-fixed) costs.

(c) Describe and illustrate the classification of material and labour costs.

(d) Prepare, and explain the nature and purpose of, profit statements in absorption and marginal costing formats.

(e) Calculate the cost and profit of a product or service.

2 Cost units, cost centres, profit centres and investment centres   Ch's 3 and 10

(a) Explain and illustrate the concept of cost units.

(b) Explain and illustrate the concept of cost centres.

(c) Explain and illustrate the concept of profit centres.

(d) Explain and illustrate the concept of investment centres.

(e) Describe performance measures appropriate to cost, profit and investment centres (cost / profit per unit / % of sales; efficiency, capacity utilisation and production volume ratios; ROCE / RI, asset turnover).

(f) Apply performance measures appropriate to cost, profit and investment centres.

       KAPLAN PUBLISHING

D RECORDING COSTS

1 Accounting for materials   Ch. 5

(a) Distinguish different types of material (raw material, work in progress and finished goods).

(b) Describe and illustrate the accounting for material costs.

(c) Calculate material requirements making allowance for sales and product/material inventory changes (control levels and EOQ are excluded).

(d) Explain and illustrate different methods used to price materials issued from inventory (FIFO, LIFO and periodic and cumulative weighted average costs).

2 Accounting for labour   Ch. 6

(a) Describe and illustrate the accounting for labour costs (including overtime premiums and idle time).

(b) Prepare an analysis of gross and net earnings.

(c) Explain and illustrate labour remuneration methods.

(d) Calculate the effect of remuneration methods and changes in productivity on unit labour costs.

3 Accounting for other expenses   Ch. 7

(a) Explain and illustrate the process of charging indirect costs to cost centres and units including cost apportionment for indirect costs (excluding reciprocal service).

(b) Explain and illustrate the process of cost absorption for indirect costs.

4 Accounting for product costs   Ch. 9

(a) Job costing

    (i) Describe the characteristics of job costing.

    (ii) Calculate unit costs using job costing.

(b) Batch costing

    (i) Describe the characteristics of batch costing.

    (ii) Calculate unit costs using batch costing.

(c) Process costing

    (i) Describe the characteristics of process costing.

    (ii) Calculate unit costs using process costing.

    (iii) Describe and illustrate the concept of equivalent units for closing work in progress.

    (iv) Calculate unit costs where there is closing work-in-progress.

    (v) Allocate process costs between finished output and work-in-progress.

    (vi) Prepare process accounts.

E THE SPREADSHEET SYSTEM

1 Spreadsheets overview   Ch. 11

(a) Explain the purposes of a spreadsheet.

(b) Describe the components of a blank spreadsheet screen.

(c) Describe methods to use/activate spreadsheet features.

(d) Describe methods of selecting ranges of cells.

(e) Explain the role of spreadsheets in management accounting.

(f) Describe the advantages and limitations of spreadsheets.

2 Creating and using spreadsheets   Ch. 11

(a) Explain factors which influence spreadsheet design and the features of a well-structured worksheet/workbook.

(b) Explain how to enter values, text and dates including automatically filling a range of cells and capturing data from another source.

(c) Identify and use formulae incorporating common arithmetic operators, use of brackets, absolute/relative cell references and simple functions (Sum, Average, Round, IF)

(d) Identify and use formulae in a workbook containing multiple worksheets and link cells from different workbooks.

(e) Describe how to move/copy and paste data and formulae.

(f) Describe, and select as appropriate, ways to edit data in a cell including the Find and Replace feature.

(g) Explain the causes of common error messages and how errors are corrected.

(h) Describe how to save, password protect and open spreadsheets

3   **Presenting and printing spreadsheet
     data/information**   Ch. 11

    (a) Describe and illustrate appropriate
        formatting features for the display of
        numbers, text, cell borders and patterns
        and for cell/worksheet protection.

    (b) Describe features which can be applied to
        rows or columns (changing height/width,
        inserting, deleting and hiding).

    (c) Describe feature which affect the on screen
        view and can be particularly useful when
        working with large worksheets/workbooks.

    (d) Use Sort and Filter to manipulate data.

    (e) Describe how charts (line, bar, pie, scatter,
        area) can be created from spreadsheet
        data and interpret the data shown.

    (f) Describe and illustrate the appropriate use
        of adding comments to a cell.

    (g) Describe how to select the output to be
        printed

    (h) Select the combination of page layout/set-
        up options to achieve an effective, user-
        friendly printed output, especially for
        worksheets containing large amounts of
        data.

THE EXAMINATION

Format of the examination

Number of marks

50 multiple-choice questions (2 marks each)   100

Time allowed: 2 hours

You must sit this subject as a computer-based exam .

Computer-based examinations

- Be sure you understand how to use the **software** before you start the exam. If in doubt, ask the assessment centre staff to explain it to you.

- Questions are **displayed on the screen** and answers are entered using keyboard and mouse. At the end of the examination, you are given a certificate showing the result you have achieved.

- **Multiple-choice questions** might ask for numerical or written answers

- **Don't panic** if you realise you've answered a question incorrectly – you can always go back and change your answer.

Answering the questions

Multiple-choice questions – read the questions carefully and work through any calculations required. This examination is biased towards narrative rather than computational questions, essentially testing knowledge rather than application.

If you don't know the answer, eliminate those options you know are incorrect and see if the answer becomes more obvious. Remember that only one answer to a multiple-choice question can be right!

If you get stuck with a question skip it and return to it later. Answer every question – if you do not know the answer, you do not lose anything by guessing. Towards the end of the examination spend the last five minutes reading through your answers and making any corrections.

Equally divide the time you spend on questions. In a two-hour examination that has 50 questions you have about 2.4 minutes per question.

Do not treat multiple-choice questions as an easy option. **Do not skip any part of the syllabus** and make sure that you have *learnt* definitions, *know* key words and their meanings and importance, and *understand* the names and meanings of rules, concepts and theories.

KAPLAN PUBLISHING

STUDY SKILLS AND REVISION GUIDANCE

Preparing to study

Set your objectives

Before starting to study decide what you want to achieve – the type of pass you wish to obtain.

This will decide the level of commitment and time you need to dedicate to your studies.

Devise a study plan

Determine when you will study.

Split these times into study sessions.

Put the sessions onto a study plan making sure you cover the course, course assignments and revision.

Stick to your plan!

Effective study techniques

Use the **SQR3** method

Survey the chapter – look at the headings and read the introduction, summary and objectives. Get an overview of what the text deals with.

Question – during the survey, ask yourself the questions that you hope the chapter will answer for you.

Read through the chapter thoroughly, answering the questions and meeting the objectives. Attempt the exercises and activities, and work through all the examples.

Recall – at the end of the chapter, try to recall the main ideas of the chapter without referring to the text. Do this a few minutes after the reading stage.

Review – check that your recall notes are correct.

Use the **MURDER** method

Mood – set the right mood.

Understand – issues covered and make note of any uncertain bits.

Recall – stop and put what you have learned into your own words.

Digest – go back and reconsider the information.

Expand – read relevant articles and newspapers.

Review – go over the material you covered to consolidate the knowledge.

While studying...

Summarise the key points of the chapter.

Make linear notes – a list of headings, divided up with subheadings listing the key points. Use different colours to highlight key points and keep topic areas together.

Try mind-maps – put the main heading in the centre of the paper and encircle it. Then draw short lines radiating from this to the main sub-headings, which again have circles around them. Continue the process from the sub-headings to sub-sub-headings, etc.

Revision

The best approach to revision is to **revise the course as you work through it**.

Also try to leave **four to six weeks before the exam for final revision**.

Make sure you **cover the whole syllabus**.

Pay special attention to **those areas where your knowledge is weak**.

If you are stuck on a topic find somebody (a tutor) to explain it to you.

Read around the subject – read good newspapers and professional journals, especially ACCA's *Student Accountant* – this can give you an advantage in the exam.

Read through the text and your notes again. Maybe put key revision points onto index cards to look at when you have a few minutes to spare.

Practise exam standard questions under timed conditions. Attempt all the different styles of questions you may be asked to answer in your exam.

Review any assignments you have completed and look at where you lost marks – put more work into those areas where you were weak.

Ensure you **know the structure of the exam** – how many questions and of what type they are.

KAPLAN PUBLISHING

Chapter 1

BUSINESS ORGANISATION

This chapter covers the organisation and main functions of an office. The chapter sets the scene for the context in which all of the operations and procedures that you will learn about in this text will take place. Later in the text you will learn more about some of the aspects mentioned in this chapter, such as materials documentation and wages analysis. The chapter covers syllabus areas A1(a) – (g)

CONTENTS

1   The main functions of an office as a centre for information and administration

2   Organisational information

3   Double-entry bookkeeping

4   Computerised accounting systems

LEARNING OUTCOMES

On completion of this chapter the student should be able to:

- Describe the organisation, and main functions, of an office as a centre for information and administration.

- Describe the function and use of a manual of policies, procedures and best practices.

- Identify the main types of transactions undertaken by a business and the key personnel involved in initiating, processing and completing transactions.

- Explain the need for effective control over transactions.

- Explain and illustrate the principles and practice of double-entry book-keeping.

- Describe and illustrate the use of ledgers and prime entry records in both integrated and interlocking accounting systems.

- Identify the key features, functions and benefits of a computerised accounting system.

1 THE MAIN FUNCTIONS OF AN OFFICE AS A CENTRE FOR INFORMATION AND ADMINISTRATION

1.1 INTRODUCTION

Every enterprise needs an office, or an area of a room designated to keeping the papers and records, because they will be involved at some point in administration. Obviously offices vary in nature and type. In manufacturing enterprises the office supports the organisation in its main task of production, whereas in commercial organisations such as banking, legal and local government, offices are concerned with supporting services rather than production.

1.2 THE FUNCTIONS OF AN OFFICE

Individual organisations all have their own procedures, rules and systems but the same type of work is done in all of them. The following diagram gives you an overview of the activities:

The office supports commerce, industry and public services by recording and providing information. Information is dealt with by an office in a variety of ways:

(a)   providing information to other organisations. This can be in different formats including price lists, quotations and financial information

(b)   receiving and processing information from other organisations

(c)   keeping records of payments made and received, wages paid to employees and debts owed by and to the organisation

(d)   providing information for internal use e.g. facts and figures for control purposes

(e)   maintaining records for future reference.

KAPLAN PUBLISHING

1.3 OFFICE ACTIVITIES

The activities include:

(a) purchasing e.g. raw materials for production, services such as electricity, items of equipment

(b) sales – this includes promoting the organisation's products or services by advertising, arranging distribution to customers, maintaining customer records, market research on customer requirements

(c) control – activities which include: effective inventory control to prevent loss of production; accurate record keeping to control costs and finances; checking documents and records for accuracy; and providing financial and statistical information through the use of computers

(d) processing information to and from the organisation, both written and spoken

(e) storing papers and documents safely using an efficient filing system

(f) presenting information by duplicating, copying, typing, word processing, charting, taping and producing various graphical and electronic formats.

(g) finance roles, such as receiving payments from customers

(h) human resource roles, such as paying staff

1.4 ADMINISTRATIVE ASSISTANTS OR CLERICAL WORKERS

Their job is to:

- record information by preparing documents

- arrange information by sorting and filing

- supply and communicate information by passing it on to relevant personnel

- keep accounts by checking the accuracy of all information that needs to be recorded within the organisation.

Conclusion The prime purpose of an office is to collect and process relevant information, which is subsequently stored or despatched to appropriate persons. Typical office activities include issuing invoices, handling purchases, dealing with customers' orders, preparing accounts and statistics, processing the payroll and other routine activities.

1.5 THE ADVANTAGES AND DISADVANTAGES OF CENTRALISED AND DECENTRALISED OFFICE FUNCTIONS

Centralisation

The challenge of a centralised office system is to make it responsive to the whole organisation. A centralised office is one where all the office procedures are done at a central point within the organisation. Larger organisations are far more likely to centralise their office services than small ones. A central general office means that a specialist section will be responsible for the provision of clerical services throughout the enterprise.

The person responsible for the management of this department will be responsible for:

(a)   advising and assisting departmental managers in the planning of clerical activities, including equipment, methods of work, supplies, personnel required and layout of office accommodation

(b)   maintaining the general office services such as mail delivery and collection, telephone and post services, central filing activities, typing pool, duplicating section and stationery storage

(c)   reviewing office machinery and equipment with a view to its maintenance and replacement.

As far as office work is concerned, centralisation is desirable for the following reasons:

•   Systems and procedures are standardised throughout the organisation, facilitating control.

•   Specialised staff can be employed and trained.

•   Expensive machinery and equipment can be purchased and used economically.

•   There is less likelihood of a backlog of work during busy periods.

•   Consultation and communication are easier and personal contact is possible.

•   It is usually more economical in terms of space and cost.

The disadvantages of centralisation include:

•   Office systems that suit one department may not suit another.

•   There is less scope for job enrichment and the lack of variety may mean that staff become bored.

•   Rigid procedures may cause difficulties in coping with emergency jobs.

•   There may be an increase in paperwork and form filling.

Decentralisation

A decentralised system is one where each department or operating division would have their own office, with all of them working, to some extent, independently of each other. Obviously, the greater the geographical distance from the centre, the greater the necessity for a decentralised office.

The benefits of decentralisation of office work include:

(a)   clerical work is better done near to the practical work to which it relates, since clerks are more likely to understand the implications of documents that they handle and are more likely to spot errors and obtain answers more easily

(b)   better service is given to department management

(c)   where promptness is essential e.g. for use on the telephone, department filing of documents is best.

The potential problems of decentralisation include the increased operational costs due to:

(a)   duplication of services; and

(b)   extra information processing.

1.6   THE STRUCTURE OF A TYPICAL OFFICE

Office organisation

The internal arrangements in an organisation depend on many factors such as:

- the size of the enterprise

- the type of work it does e.g. manufacturing or service sector industry

- the number of employees

- whether it is involved in exporting.

A small organisation, especially in the service sector, may only have a few employees but in a technically complex organisation there is more specialisation of function, with each employee concentrating on his or her own specific job. The layout is usually shown on an organisation chart, which is a diagram illustrating the structure of an organisation.

Definition   An **organisation chart** is a diagram of the formal relationships and communication flow between positions within an organisation.

It defines not only the main parts of the enterprise, but also:

- names of individuals in specific key roles

- line structure (i.e. who reports to whom)

- levels of authority and responsibility

- supervisory structure

- lines of essential communication.

Knowing where people are and what they do allows:

- more efficient communication

- accurate delivery of mail

- the prompt transfer of phone calls to the right person; and

- effective handling of queries.

An enterprise may be sub-divided into production, sales and marketing, research and development (R&D), Human Resources (personnel), finance, purchasing, legal and secretarial, information processing, information technology (IT) and industrial relations. An example of an organisation chart is shown next:

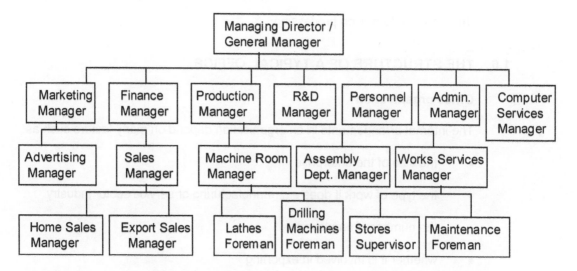

Conclusion   The internal arrangements in an organisation depend on the size of the enterprise, the type of work it does, the number of employees and whether it exports its products or services.

Personnel involved

If we think of a large organisation which is split into many departments, the typical job titles and functions within each department could give us an idea of the type and size of office required to accommodate the job holders. Starting at the top of our organisation chart:

The *Managing Director* or General Manager will co-ordinate the work of the other managers and is responsible to the Board of Directors for the effective running of the organisation.

The *Marketing Manager* will have overall responsibility for a number of staff including:

- sales managers, which may be domestic or export and may be divided further into continents e.g. Asia, Africa, South America

- advertising manager

- distribution manager

- order assistants

- shipping assistants

- sales representatives

- transport assistants.

The types of function within this department or office include keeping customer records, market research, advertising, sales promotion, public relations, preparation of sales documentation e.g. price lists, quotations, customer liaison, exhibitions and trade fairs representation, warehousing and distribution of goods.

The *Finance Manager* will be responsible for all the financial affairs of the organisation and may have the following staff:

- financial accountant

- cost accountant

- management accountant

- chief cashier

- assistant positions for wages, costing, ledgers and credit control.

The work done in this department includes: issuing invoices, credit notes and statements; recording money inwards; paying cheques and recording money outwards; wages; expense claims and petty cash; producing company accounts; costing; and producing management information of a financial nature.

The *Production Manager* is responsible for the production of goods, the maintenance of equipment, quality control, inventory control, work study, production planning and control, stores control and despatch. The type of job title within this department will vary tremendously according to the type of goods being made and may include:

- works manager

- engineers

- draughtsmen

- production planners

- supervisors

- stores staff

- factory operatives

- despatch assistants.

The *Research and Development Manager* has overall responsibility for the design, development and testing of new products and also the improvement of existing products. He or she will also need to keep abreast of technological developments. The staff may include designers and engineers and the type of staff will reflect the needs of the company e.g. R&D in a pharmaceutical environment will use different skills from those that are used in a car manufacturer.

The *Human Resources Manager* (sometimes called the Personnel Manager) has a wide departmental role which may include the following responsibilities:

- recruitment, selection and induction of staff

- personnel record keeping

- staff appraisals

- salary grading schemes

- dismissals and redundancies

- training

- welfare

- industrial relations and trade union negotiations.

The types of staff required to fulfil these roles include: training officers, welfare officers, security staff, nurses and canteen staff.

The *Administrative Manager* may be the Company Secretary or the Chief Administrative Officer and will have responsibility for all the legal affairs of the organisation. This will include insurance, dealing with shareholders, organising company meetings, office planning, office systems and services e.g. telephone services, reprographic services and telecommunications. Staff may include caretakers and cleaners.

The *Computer Services Manager* and his or her staff will be responsible for designing computer systems for existing operations and identifying new areas and future needs for computerisation. The types of staff may include systems analysts, programmers and data preparation operators. Apart from programming, the staff will provide computer services to the organisation on a day-to-day basis and assist management decision making.

ACTIVITY 1

If the organisation has a purchasing department, what would be the functions within the department and what type of staff would you expect to be employed in it?

For a suggested answer, see the 'Answers' section at the end of the book.

Office site

The location of the office needs careful consideration. There must be enough space for employees and equipment and also for expansion in the future. The organisation must decide whether to locate office services near to manufacturing or sales departments or near to customers for convenience.

Other considerations include whether it is necessary to have proximity to banks and transport facilities.

Layout of office

Some points to note when studying the layout of the office/department:

- large open spaces are deemed to be better than a series of small rooms

- natural light should be used where possible

- the layout should facilitate the flow of work

- noisy machines may distract and should be kept out of general offices if possible.

Another factor is the use of colour in the decoration, which can influence morale and efficiency. There are also statutory requirements which must be considered covering such things as temperature, space per worker, ventilation, lighting, facilities for washing and eating, fencing of machinery, first aid and fire precautions.

The designs of offices fall into three main categories:

(a)   *Open plan* – most offices are open plan. It is where a large number of employees are together in one large office. The advantages of this design include:

- changes in the layout and location of individual members of staff can be easily made

- communication is easier than if a number of smaller offices exists, making it easier to see whether an individual is in or out of the office

- efficient supervision and even distribution of work is made possible

- machines and equipment can be used efficiently

- cheaper maintenance and cleaning costs because there are no interior walls.

There can be disadvantages to the open plan office unless efforts are made to overcome them. For example:

- management can become involved in routine matters

- absence of own office status symbol tends to lower the morale of ambitious staff

- noise can be a problem but can be reduced with insulation materials and fitted carpets

- discussion between office employees can disturb employees working nearby

- lack of privacy can be annoying and may possibly reduce efficiency. A separate interview room can overcome some of the problems, allowing visitors to be received and personal staff matters to be dealt with privately.

Conclusion   The main arguments in favour of open planning are increased flexibility of layout, economies of cost in building and running and easier communication, administration and supervision.

(b)   Landscaped offices – are supposed to address the problems of the open plan office. This type of office has a high standard of equipment and furnishings. The desks are placed in a rather random fashion and the use of acoustic screens, filing cabinets and plants breaks up the floor area. Status is served by allocating more space and better furnishings to certain staff. Noise and distractions are greatly reduced by the arrangement of equipment.

(c)   Corridor – are found in older buildings and, as you would guess from the name of them, are separate offices leading off a corridor. They are generally partitioned off with walls but variations do exist e.g. half glazed. The major advantage of this type of office is the privacy and quiet.

The main disadvantages will include the fact that it does not promote team working and supervision of staff could be more difficult.

2 ORGANISATIONAL INFORMATION

2.1 EXAMPLES OF ORGANISATIONAL INFORMATION

The flow of information within an organisation involves the communication of parts of that information to interested parties. Organisational information includes:

- organisation charts
- personnel files
- internal telephone list
- staff planning charts
- holiday rota
- notice boards
- company magazine
- company handbook
- manual of best practice/procedures.

2.2 PURPOSE OF THE MANUAL OF BEST PRACTICE /PROCEDURES

Although they are not always immediately apparent, every office has systems which are usually referred to as 'office procedures'. Procedures represent the summation of a series of operations necessary to perform a task associated with the receipt, recording, arrangement, storage, security and communication of information. The establishment of systems and procedures will ensure that organisational objectives are attained and will help to ensure that there is effective control over transactions.

Data and information are constantly flowing within an organisation, some being generated internally and some stemming from external sources. All of this information must be processed i.e. dealt with in the appropriate manner in relation to the type and nature of that information. To aid this goal and to ensure that it is attained in the most effective, efficient and economical manner, a system needs to be established. That system will involve activities and procedures for processing and above all the documents needed to convey the information to the right people and to control the activities.

As with most aspects of business administration, there are certain principles which have been built up over a long period as being the most effective. These principles would have evolved naturally by trial and error or by the application of formal or informal research designed to produce solutions to particular problem areas. The principles that are generally recognised are equally applicable to the checking of existing procedures and to any alteration to those existing procedures or to the introduction of new procedures.

Those principles and guidelines include the following:

(a) There should be a smooth flow of work with no bottlenecks.

(b) Movement of staff should be kept to a minimum.

(c) Duplication of work should be avoided.

(d) The best and most effective use of existing specialist attributes should be made.

(e)   Simplicity within systems should be sought. Complications usually lead to misinterpretations and/or mistakes.

(f)   Human efforts should be aided by machines where appropriate.

(g)   Any system must be cost-effective. The benefits should be compared with the cost of implementation and subsequent supervision costs.

The benefit of implementing procedures and systems will be even greater if they are formalised in writing. This is normally achieved by the preparation of 'laid-down' or written procedures in either an office procedure manual, or in the form of a duty list issued to staff. The written instructions will indicate clearly what is required to be done, when, where and how. They will additionally incorporate details of the interaction of procedures within the system as a whole.

ACTIVITY 2

Can you think of some advantages and disadvantages with the preparation of procedure manuals?

For a suggested answer, see the 'Answers' section at the end of the book.

2.3   EXERCISING CONTROL OVER TRANSACTIONS

Our earlier discussions of all of the different roles undertaken by personnel in a large organisation should have helped you to realise that a large number of transactions are undertaken each day within a business.

It is vital that effective control is exercised over these transactions and the manual of policies and procedures can assist with this. Examples of the types of transaction that require effective control are as follows:

(a)   Placing orders with suppliers. This transaction creates a legally binding agreement between the supplier and the organisation. Therefore it is important that procedures for the selection of suppliers are documented and that only authorised people are permitted to place orders. One way to ensure this is to have all orders raised using prenumbered order forms. Blank forms should be kept safe and in the custody of authorised staff. Outgoing forms should be signed by a supervisor in the buying department who can check that there is a good business case for raising the order.

(b)   Supplying goods and services to a customer on credit. Appropriate procedures must be followed in checking the customer's creditworthiness otherwise the organisation may be unable to recover the money owed to them. New customers might be checked by requesting references from existing suppliers or their bank. Established customers might have their accounts reviewed prior to any further sale to ensure that they are settling their invoices on time.

(c)   Receiving goods into store from a supplier. Procedures should be described, for example, concerning the documentation to be completed to record the receipt of goods and to ensure that the supplier is paid for the delivery. Staff checking incoming goods should make a record on a prenumbered goods received note. This should be passed to the accounts department to enable the accounts payable staff to compare the quantities stated on the supplier's invoice before settlement.

(d)   Payment of a supplier. Only authorised people should be able to pay money to a supplier and the procedures for authorisation of a payment should be carefully documented. For example, staff authorised to prepare and handle cheques should not be involved with maintaining records of accounts payable. That would make it far more difficult to prepare a cheque for personal use and then record it as a payment to a supplier.

(e)   Payment of employees. Only bone fide staff should be paid and they must be paid at the correct hourly or monthly rates. A personnel department, which is independent of the payroll department, might keep the staffing records, along with the pay grades of each individual member of staff.

3   DOUBLE-ENTRY BOOKKEEPING

3.1   INTRODUCTION

Accounting is concerned with expressing and summarising in monetary terms the various economic transactions undertaken by an organisation. Accounting theory is based on the concept of balancing the accounting equation:

assets – liabilities = capital + profits

Double-entry bookkeeping is a means of controlling the accounting records in such a way that the accounting equation (i.e. effectively the balance sheet) remains in balance. As a method it is based on every transaction having two equal sides to it.

Example

Buying product A for $500

The double entry is to increase inventory by $500   (add to assets)

and decrease cash by $500   (reduce assets)

then selling Product A for $550

The double entry is to increase cash by $550   (add to assets)

decrease inventory by $500   (reduce assets)

increase profits by $50   (increase profits)

3.2   BOOKS OF PRIME ENTRY

Businesses typically undertake many transactions every day so it would be impractical to record each transaction separately as it arises. Therefore the details of most individual transactions are entered in a book of prime entry first. These are then summarised on a regular basis and the summarised information is posted to ledger accounts in an accounting system.

The main books of prime entry are:

*   Purchases day book – this is a list of each credit purchase made during the period, showing the date, supplier, and the amounts (net value, Sales Tax and total). The total values of net purchases, Sales Tax and total due can then be determined and recorded.

*   Purchases returns day book – records all purchases credit notes received in the period. The details recorded are the same as for the purchases day book.

- Sales day book – records all credit sales invoices made during the period. This is similar to the details in the purchases day book. The date, customer name, net, Sales Tax and gross values of each transaction are listed and totalled regularly.

- Cash book – records all bank transactions on a day to day basis. Columns can be used to analyse the payments so that it is possible to keep track of, say, totals paid to suppliers, payrolls, receipts from customers and any other regular receipts and payments.

- Petty cash book – records all cash transactions such as reimbursement of staff travelling expenses and any minor cash purchases. Again, these can be analysed by having separate columns for specific types of transaction.

- Wages/salaries book – records the detail of wages and salaries such as the date, payee, gross wage or salary, deductions for tax, pension, etc., and net wage/salary.

- Journal – records all infrequently occurring transactions such as correcting errors, writing off a bad debt, etc.

Controls are exercised over the accuracy and completeness of recording of transactions entered in the books of prime entry by maintaining control accounts in the ledger which are reconciled to the books of prime entry and by performing external reconciliations such as the bank reconciliation to control the cash book and use of the bank account.

The data captured in the books of prime entry feeds into two separate information systems. The **financial accounting** system is used to keep track of the overall financial position of the enterprise and its performance, measured in historical terms. The main function of the financial accounting records is to enable the preparation of financial statements for external reporting purposes. The **costing/management accounting** system is used to keep track of the details of costs and revenues so that they can be monitored and controlled. Costing records are usually designed to highlight areas where there are deviations from plans, such as overspending on a particular material, so that they can be corrected as quickly as possible.

3.3 COST BOOKKEEPING

There are typically two approaches to cost bookkeeping. Some businesses maintain records for cost accounting separately (interlocking accounts), whereas other do so as part of the overall accounting systems (integrated accounts).

Interlocking accounts

Definition **Interlocking accounts** are a system in which the cost accounts are distinct from the financial accounts, the two sets of accounts being kept continuously in agreement by the use of control accounts.

The cost ledger control account

In an interlocking system the cost accounts will only need to record the transactions relating to the costs and revenue of the business. Details of cash, receivables, payables and capital are part of the financial accounting routine and are ignored for costing purposes. However in order to maintain the double entry in full, organisations will often have a cost ledger control account in which all entries that would have been to cash, receivables, payables or capital are made.

Integrated accounts

Definition   **Integrated accounts** are a set of accounts in which the cost accounts and financial accounts are combined in one system using the same data for all accounting purposes.

In the example which follows we will demonstrate the operation of an interlocking system. If an integrated system was used instead the main accounting principles would be the same. The only difference would be that, instead of making entries into the cost ledger control account, in an integrated system the relevant entries would be made in the accounts for payables, or for receivables and so on.

3.4   RECORDING THE PURCHASE OF INVENTORY

When inventory is received from suppliers the purchases must be entered into the cost accounts.

The **double entry** for the purchase of goods/materials is:

DR Stores control account

CR Cost ledger control account (CLCA)

The amount recorded will be the net of Sales Tax invoice value taken from the supplier's invoice.

Example

Suppose that a purchase of 500 units of material X is received into stores with a total invoice value of $11,750 and a net of Sales Tax total of $10,000. The entry for this must be made in the stores control account.

Solution

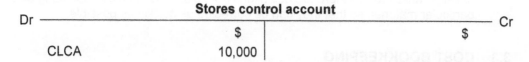

Dr		Stores control account		Cr
		$		$
CLCA		10,000		

The entry is net of Sales Tax as the Sales Tax is not a cost to the business – it will be reclaimed from Revenue & Customs (in the United Kingdom). The credit side of this entry is to the cost ledger control account.

Transaction detail

This of course only tells us that a purchase of $10,000 of materials has been made; there is no information about what material it is or what quantity of material was purchased. This information can be obtained from the detailed subsidiary ledger, the material inventory account for material X.

MATERIAL INVENTORY ACCOUNT

MATERIAL X

Material: ....   Maximum quantity: ....

X

Code: ....   Minimum quantity: ....

Receipts					Issues					Inventory		
Date	GRN no.	Quantity	Unit price	Amount	Date	Stores req.	Quantity	Unit price	Amount	Quantity	Unit price	Amount
			$	$		no.		$	$		$	$
		500	20.00	10,000						500	20.00	10,000

The stores department will also keep a less detailed record of all receipts and issues of inventory on a bin card. Stores staff have no need to know the value of the goods that they handle, but they do need to be aware of the quantities on hand so that they can warn the buying department when inventory levels of any particular item are running low. The information on the bin card will be similar to that of the material inventory account, except that there will be no reference to monetary values. The bin card might carry information about the location of the item in the stores.

3.5 RECORDING THE ISSUE OF MATERIALS

When the factory sends a materials requisition form to stores, stores issues those materials required to the factory. The bin card and material inventory account will be written up to show the issue and an entry must also be made in the cost accounts.

The double entry will depend on whether or not the materials are 'direct' or 'indirect'. This distinction is covered in more detail in later chapters but for now we will limit ourselves to the following:

- Direct costs can directly identified with a specific cost unit. For example, if making a wooden chair, then the cost of the wood would be a direct cost as the cost of wood could be matched to specific chairs.

- Indirect costs cannot be easily identified with a specific cost unit. For example, oil used in the machinery to make the chairs would be difficult to match to individual chairs made.

Indirect costs are also known as 'overheads'.

Double entry

The double entry for the issue of materials/goods is:

DR   Work in progress control account (WIP control account) for direct materials

DR   Production overheads control account for indirect materials

CR   Stores control account

The work in progress control account is effectively the factory accounts as it will be used to record all of the costs relating to the factory.

Example

The factory issues a materials requisition for 200 units of direct material X which will be valued at $20 per unit by stores, the unit cost of this consignment of material X ($10,000/500).

Write up the cost accounts and the material inventory account.

Solution

Stores control account

Dr		$			$	Cr
	CLCA	10,000	WIP control (200 × $20)		4,000	

Work in progress control account

Dr		$		$	Cr
	Stores	4,000			

MATERIAL INVENTORY ACCOUNT

MATERIAL X

Material: ....   Maximum quantity: ....

Code: ....X.................................   Minimum quantity: ....

Receipts					Issues					Inventory		
Date	GRN no.	Quantity	Unit price $	Amount $	Date	Stores req. no.	Quantity	Unit price $	Amount $	Quantity	Unit price $	Amount $
		500	20.00	10,000						500	20.00	10,000
							200	20.00	4,000	300	20.00	6,000

3.6 ACCOUNTING FOR WAGES AND SALARIES

Double entry

When the wages and salaries for the period are calculated by the payroll department the initial double entry for the total wage bill is:

DR   Gross wages control account

CR   Cost ledger control account

Example

Suppose that the total wages for the period are $6,000. Enter this figure in the cost accounts.

Solution

Gross wages control account

Dr		$			$	Cr
	CLCA	6,000				

Analysis of wages

The payroll department will have analysed the total wage bill for costing purposes to show which departments should be allocated the wages cost. As with materials, wages would be analysed into direct or indirect as well as whether they belong to the wages cost for the factory, the selling function and/or administration.

The double entry would then be:

DR   WIP control account – with factory employees' direct wages

DR   Production overheads control account – with factory employees' indirect wages

DR   Selling function – with sales personnel's wages

DR   Administration – with administration personnel's wages

CR   Gross wages control

Example

Continuing our example from above suppose that the $6,000 of wages cost is analysed by payroll as follows:

	$
Factory direct wages	3,000
Selling function	2,000
Administration	1,000
	–––––
	6,000
	–––––

Write up the cost accounting records.

Solution

Gross wages control account

Dr		$		$	Cr
CLCA		6,000	WIP control	3,000	
			Selling function	2,000	
			Administration	1,000	

Work in progress control account

Dr		$		$	Cr
Stores		4,000			
Gross wages control		3,000			

Selling function control account

Dr		$		$	Cr
Gross wages control		2,000			

Administration control account

Dr		$		$	Cr
Gross wages control		1,000			

3.7 OTHER EXPENSES

Expense invoices

When invoices for other expenses are received, they must be coded so that they are recognised as belonging to the correct department and whether or not they are direct or indirect. In general the expenses will be manufacturing (factory), selling or administration and will be overheads.

Double entry

The double entry for these expenses will be as follows:

DR Production overheads control account

DR Selling function control account

DR Administration control account

CR Cost ledger control account

The production overheads are part of the factory manufacturing costs but they are kept separately in a production overheads control account at this stage as there is more accounting to be done with these overheads.

Example

Continuing our example from above, suppose that the coded expense invoices show that production expenses for the period were $6,000, selling expenses $400 and administration expenses $500.

Enter these into the cost accounts.

Solution

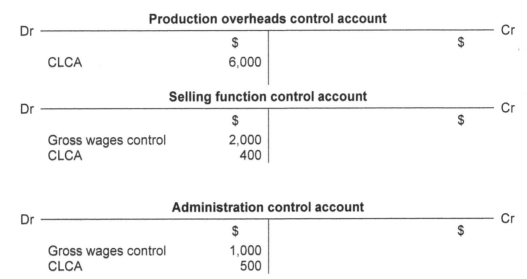

Production overheads control account

Dr		$		$	Cr
CLCA		6,000			

Selling function control account

Dr		$		$	Cr
Gross wages control		2,000			
CLCA		400			

Administration control account

Dr		$		$	Cr
Gross wages control		1,000			
CLCA		500			

4 COMPUTERISED ACCOUNTING SYSTEMS

4.1 THE EFFECTS OF COMPUTERISING THE ACCOUNTING SYSTEM

It is possible to record all transactions and prepare management information on a manual basis and for very small or simple businesses this will still be the norm. However, computerising the accounting system will have an enormous effect on, and should be an enormous benefit to, the majority of businesses.

The main effects are:

- **Routine processing** – processing of routine transactions can be done in bigger volumes, at greater speed and with greater accuracy. Most business transactions fall into a small number of types – making sales, buying goods, making payments, receiving payments, etc. – and therefore computerising the accounting system takes away the labour intensity of a manual system and minimises the possibility of human error.

- **Paperless office** – the handling and storing of data electronically will reduce the need to use and store paper.

- **Information access** – managers are likely to have access to more accurate, reliable and up to date information. The ways of cutting the data from a database can provide considerably more analysis of the information. Timescales will reduce from weeks to hours.

- **Planning activities** – the ready access of accurate, reliable data should allow a more thorough level of planning and enable the use of spreadsheets to be integrated into the planning process for budgeting purposes.

- **Control** – the need for reconciliations will be minimised and much of the desirable reconciliations can be fully automated as well. Information for other control purposes will be readily available and can be integrated into the accounting system, e.g. prompt letters for overdue payment can be automatically produced from the records.

- **Decision making** – decision support system, sensitivity models can be integrated giving management a greater width and depth of decision-making information.

- **Communication and sharing of information** – this can be supported by networking locally and by allowing local and head office access to localised data. This can be usefully exploited by multi-site organisations and, for example, where inventory is stored on multi-sites.

- **Motivation** – it takes away most of the mundane aspects of work and allows employees to spend more time on analysing and using the information rather than processing.

4.2 RECORDING TRANSACTIONS IN A COMPUTERISED SYSTEM

In a computerised accounting system a file is a collection of similar records, for example a receivables file or a payables file. Within each file there will be a number of records, for example one customer account in the receivables file would be one record. There will be a record for each customer on the file.

Within each record there will be a number of fields. Each field contains an item of data about the particular record. For example in a single customer record there will be a field for customer number, a field for customer name, another for customer address, one for the amount owed by the customer and so on.

There are two main ways in which data can be recorded or processed in a computerised system: batch processing and real-time processing.

4.3 BATCH PROCESSING

In a batch processing system the data is collected together and stored until it is processed in batches at regular intervals, for example weekly or monthly and so on. For example a company might process its payroll weekly or monthly.

Advantages of batch processing include the following:

- It is easier to control and check the transactions because the processing of the data occurs at definite times.

- Batches can be processed at times when the computer is less busy on other tasks, for example in the evening after the majority of staff have gone home.

The main disadvantage of batch processing is that, since the data is not processed immediately, the information provided by the system at any point in time may be out of date. This can present particular problems in some situations, for example when dealing with customer queries about their account balance or about the availability of certain items of inventory.

4.4   REAL-TIME PROCESSING

In a real-time system data is input and processed immediately, instead of being stored for processing at pre-determined times as in batch processing. This means that the information provided by the system is always up to date. In some systems the input or the processing of new data might be delayed slightly, in which case the system would be referred to as on-line. However as we shall see in the next chapter a real-time system can result in some particular security issues.

4.5   INTEGRATED COMPUTERISED ACCOUNTING SYSTEMS

Most computerised accounting systems are integrated systems. This means that a single entry into the system will update all relevant records. For example when a payment is made to a supplier a single entry into the integrated system will do the following:

- Update the supplier's individual account in the purchase ledger.

- Update the bank account in the nominal ledger.

- Update the payables control account in the nominal ledger.

Advantages of an integrated system include the following:

- Data needs to be entered only once to update all the relevant records.

- The system is more efficient because there is no need to quit one application to access another.

- Possible human error in forgetting to update a relevant record is reduced.

- The system is easy for users to understand, since all the components of the package will have similar screen layouts and functions. As well as reducing training costs the incidence of user errors should be reduced.

- Integrating the records of the various departments means that information can be more accurate and up to date. For example in an integrated system the processing of a sales invoice simultaneously updates the inventory record. This means that inventory levels can be monitored more efficiently.

CONCLUSION

You should now have an appreciation of the main transactions carried out in an organisation and the personnel who may be involved in carrying out these transactions.

KEY TERMS

Organisation chart – a diagram of the formal relationships and communication flow between positions within an organisation.

Procedures manual – written procedures of the operations required to perform tasks in an organisation.

Books of prime entry – detailed record of transactions undertaken.

Interlocking accounts – a system in which the cost accounts are distinct from the financial accounts, the two sets of accounts being kept continuously in agreement by the use of a cost ledger control account.

Integrated accounts – a set of accounts in which the cost accounts and financial accounts are maintained in one system using the same data for all accounting purposes.

Batch processing – in a batch processing system the data is collected together and stored until it is processed in batches at regular intervals, for example weekly or monthly and so on.

Real-time system – in a real-time system data is input and processed immediately.

SELF TEST QUESTIONS

Paragraph

1	Outline the main functions of an office.	1.2
2	Draw a simple organisation chart.	1.6
3	Describe the purpose of a procedures manual.	2.2
4	Name three books of prime entry.	3.2
5	In a computerised system, distinguish between a file, a field and a record.	4.2
6	Distinguish between a batch processing system and a real-time system.	4.3, 4.4

EXAM-STYLE QUESTIONS

1   Which one of the statements below does not describe one of the advantages of centralisation of office work?

    A   It is usually more economical in terms of space and cost.

    B   Expensive machinery and equipment can be purchased and used economically.

    C   Specialised staff can be employed.

    D   Better service is given to department management.

2   Which of the following employees in an organisation is the finance manager unlikely to have responsibility for?

    A   Cost accountant

    B   Chief cashier

    C   Wages clerk

    D   Transport clerk

3   What is a book of prime entry?

    A   A ledger account where transactions are originally recorded

    B   A record in which transactions are originally recorded before being transferred to a ledger account

    C   A separate ledger where details of a particular type of transaction are recorded in parallel to the recording in the nominal ledger

    D   A set of memorandum ledger accounts which back up the total figures recorded in the nominal ledger

4   In an integrated accounting system, which of the following is the correct double entry for an administration expense incurred on credit?

    A   DR   Administration expense control account

            CR   Cost ledger control account

    B   DR   Administration expense control account

            CR   Payables control account

    C   DR   Administration expense control account

            CR   Cash account

    D   DR   Payables control account

            CR   Administration expense control account

For suggested answers, see the 'Answers' section at the end of the book.

Chapter 2

INTRODUCTION TO MANAGEMENT INFORMATION

This introductory chapter sets the scene for your further studies of management information. It covers the differences between management accounting and financial accounting and then goes on to look at cost centres, profit centres and investment centres. The chapter covers syllabus areas A2 (a – g) and C2 (a – d).

CONTENTS

1   The purpose of management information

2   The sources and categories of information

3   Management accounting and financial accounting

4   Responsibility centres

5   Cost units

LEARNING OUTCOMES

On completion of this chapter the student should be able to:

- State the purpose of management information.

- Compare cost and management accounting with external financial reporting.

- Distinguish between data and information.

- Describe the features of useful management information.

- Describe and identify sources and categories of information.

- Explain the limitations of cost and management accounting information.

- Describe the role of a trainee accountant in a cost and management accounting system.

- Explain and illustrate the concept of cost centres

- Explain and illustrate the concept of profit centres

- Explain and illustrate the concept of investment centres

- Explain and illustrate the concept of cost units.

1 THE PURPOSE OF MANAGEMENT INFORMATION

1.1 WHAT IS A MANAGER?

A manager in an organisation can include anyone who is involved in the decision-making processes, and in the planning and controlling of the organisation's activities. There are different levels of management, for example the managing director is at a higher level than the line manager of the production department. The types of decision taken by each of these managers is very different, therefore the information requirements of the managers will be different. Managers need useful information (management information) in order to make decisions, to plan and to control the activities of the company. **Management accountants** provide managers with this information.

1.2 DECISION MAKING

In the course of running a business, management will be faced with many decisions. These will include both **long-term decisions** about the future direction of the business and **short-term decisions** about the day-to-day running of the organisation.

Examples of **long-term,** or strategic, decisions that managers may make include:

(a) which products to continue to produce and sell based upon factors such as the profitability and market share of those products

(b) which products to withdraw from manufacturing and selling

(c) how many staff to employ – whether there should be a reduction in the number of employees or whether more staff should be recruited

(d) whether or not to invest in new machinery and equipment.

Other **day-to-day** or operational decisions that might have to be made include:

(a) which products to make and the detailed scheduling of production activities

(b) how much overtime is required to meet output requirements

(c) how much inventory to hold, taking into account the cost of holding inventory compared with the cost of placing frequent orders and the risk of running out of inventory completely.

Data and information

Data consist of raw facts and statistics before they have been processed. Once data has been processed into a useful form, appropriate to the needs of the user, it is called **information**.

Useful management information enables managers to make **informed decisions**. This does not mean the managers will definitely make the right decisions or those that are necessarily the best for the business. Information is simply an aid to the decision-making process.

KAPLAN PUBLISHING

ACTIVITY 1

Think about the kind of decisions that are made in your organisation or in one you have worked for in the past. Which were long-term decisions and which were day-to-day or operational decisions?

There is no feedback to this activity.

1.3 PLANNING

The management of an organisation will spend much of its time looking forward and planning the longer-term operations and strategies of the organisation. In order to be able to plan how to operate successfully in the future, managers will need current, detailed information about the organisation.

Management will need to make detailed plans. These plans may include how many of each type of product to make and sell, what these products will cost to make, how many employees are required to make the products and how much they must be paid. These detailed plans are expressed in financial terms in the organisation's **budgets**.

In order to prepare these budgets, managers will need to know what each product costs to manufacture or how much it costs to provide a particular service to customers in order to decide which products or services to continue producing. They will need to know how productive the various employees or work groups are in order to concentrate efforts on improving productivity. They will need to know how much has been spent on advertising in the past in order to determine how much should be spent in the future.

1.4 CONTROL

As well as making plans for the future management will also be concerned with whether the plans and budgets for the current period are being achieved. Regular comparison of actual costs and income with those that were anticipated in the budget for the period enables managers to identify where control action may be necessary. Control action might be taken in order to bring actual performance back into line with the budget, or if this is not possible then it may be necessary to prepare a revised budget. This new budget is then used to continue to exercise control, by regular comparison of the actual results with the revised budget.

1.5 THE FEATURES OF EFFECTIVE MANAGEMENT INFORMATION

For management information to be useful and effective it must have a number of qualities. Cost and management accounting information systems should be designed to produce information with all of the following desirable qualities although this may not be possible in all cases.

Relevant

The information must be relevant to the needs of the users. The provision of irrelevant information wastes time and money and there is a risk that relevant information might be overlooked if the manager is required to search for the relevant items.

- **Difficulty:** if there are a variety of users it can be difficult to identify the needs of each individual.

Reliable

The information should be of a standard that can be depended upon by users when they are making their decisions.

- **Difficulty:** the complexities of modern business make reliability difficult to achieve in all cases.

Understandable

The information should be understandable by the user. Excessive use of jargon must be avoided and the level of complexity of the information should be appropriate to the skill and knowledge of the manager who is using it.

- **Difficulty:** users may have differing levels of ability.

Complete

The user must be provided with all the information necessary to make decisions and plan and control activities.

- **Difficulty:** there can be a conflict between completeness and relevance. It can be difficult to ensure completeness without overwhelming the user with too much information.

Accurate

Linked to the requirement for reliability, information must be accurate otherwise incorrect actions might be taken based on inaccurate information.

- **Difficulty:** it is usually necessary to determine a *sufficient* level of accuracy. Depending on the type of information, perfect accuracy is not always possible or necessary. For example figures may be rounded to the nearest hundred or to the nearest thousand.

Timely

Information that is provided late will be less effective as any action based on the information may be taken too late.

- **Difficulty:** there can be a conflict between timeliness and accuracy. Information that is provided very rapidly will usually of necessity include a number of estimates.

Clear

Information must be communicated in a way which is clear and easily understood by the user. For example tables should be used where appropriate.

- **Difficulty:** the differing ability levels of users of the information may mean that some can easily understand a technical diagram whereas other users of the information might require a longer, narrative explanation.

Consistent

The same principles should be applied in preparing consecutive management reports so that comparisons are possible between different periods.

- **Difficulty:** a focus on consistency might introduce an element of rigidity into the management reporting processes.

Cost effective

Management information is not effective if the cost of obtaining it is more than the benefits it is expected to provide. This point is linked to the need for *sufficient* accuracy and timeliness. Information that is perfectly accurate and which takes a long time to produce may be so expensive that its cost outweighs any savings or benefits derived from decisions based on that information.

- **Difficulty**: until the information is ready for use it can be difficult to determine whether it will generate sufficient benefits or savings to cover its cost.

2 THE SOURCES AND CATEGORIES OF INFORMATION

Information may be based on primary data or on secondary data and may be obtained from internal sources or from external sources.

2.1 PRIMARY DATA AND SECONDARY DATA

Primary data is gathered for a specific purpose. For example a company might interview its own customers directly to find out more about their buying habits.

Secondary data is not originally gathered for a single purpose but may be used in a variety of ways. For example instead of interviewing customers directly (gathering primary data) a company might use a secondary source of data such as published government statistics in order to investigate customer buying patterns.

2.2 INTERNAL SOURCES OF INFORMATION

Internal sources of information come from within the organisation itself, for example from the personnel records or from the financial accounting records.

Examples of internal information include the following:

- The rate of pay for employees with appropriate skills might be provided by the personnel department when a new product is being costed.
- In an accountancy firm detailed time records might be provided by the auditing department to assist in preparing invoices for audit work completed.

2.3 EXTERNAL SOURCES OF INFORMATION

External information comes from sources outside the organisation.

Examples of external information include the following:

- Consumer price index statistics
- Health and Safety legislation
- Financial Reporting Standards.

3 MANAGEMENT ACCOUNTING AND FINANCIAL ACCOUNTING

Financial accounting information and **management accounting** information will both use the same basic data but they will be presented differently and will fulfil different roles.

3.1 FINANCIAL ACCOUNTING

The **financial accounts** record transactions between the business and its customers, suppliers, employees and owners. The managers of the business must account for the way in which funds entrusted to them have been used and, therefore, records of assets and liabilities are needed as well as a statement of any increase in the total wealth of the business. Financial accounts are presented in the form of an **income statement** and a **balance sheet**.

Definition   **Financial accounting** is:

- the classification and recording of monetary transactions; and

- the presentation and interpretation of the results of those transactions in order to assess performance over a period and the financial position at a given date.

3.2 COST ACCOUNTING

Cost accounting involves applying a set of principles, methods and techniques to determine and analyse costs within the separate units of a business.

Definition   The establishment of budgets, standard costs and actual costs of operations, processes, activities or products; and the analysis of variances, profitability or the social use of funds.

3.3 MANAGEMENT ACCOUNTING

Management accounting is a wider concept involving **professional knowledge and skill** in the preparation and presentation of information to all levels of management in an organisation. The source of such information is the financial and cost accounts. The information is intended to assist management in decision making and in the planning and control of activities in both the short and long term.

Definition   An integral part of management concerned with identifying, presenting and interpreting information which is used for formulating strategy, planning and control, decision making and optimising the use of resources.

3.4 INVOLVEMENT WITH MANAGEMENT

Financial accounting, cost accounting and management accounting involve participation in management to ensure that there is effective:

- formulation of plans to meet objectives

- formulation of short-term operational plans

- acquisition and use of finance and recording of actual transactions

- communication of financial and operating information

- corrective action to bring plans and results into line

- reviewing and reporting on systems and operations.

3.5 FINANCIAL ACCOUNTS AND MANAGEMENT INFORMATION

It may be helpful to look at a simple income statement to see the role of management accounting:

XYZ Company
Income statement for period X

	$	$
Turnover		200,000
Cost of sales:		
Materials consumed	80,000	
Wages	40,000	
Production expenses	15,000	
	———	135,000
Gross profit		65,000
Marketing expenses	15,000	
General administrative expenses	10,000	
Financing costs	4,000	
	———	29,000
Net profit		36,000

This statement may be adequate to provide outsiders with an overview of the trading results of the whole business, but managers would need much more detail to answer questions such as:

- What are the major products and are they profitable?

- By how much has inventory of raw materials increased?

- How does the labour cost per unit compare with the cost for last period?

- Is the expenditure incurred by the personnel department higher than expected?

The management accounting system reports will provide the answers to these (and many other) questions on a regular basis. In addition, the management accounts will contain detailed information concerning raw materials inventory, work in progress and finished goods as a basis for the valuation necessary to prepare periodic and final accounts.

3.6 THE RELATIONSHIP BETWEEN COST AND MANAGEMENT ACCOUNTS AND FINANCIAL ACCOUNTS

Financial accounting information and cost and management accounting information come from the same sources but are presented differently. For example the cost of purchases for a week will be found in the financial accounting records from the purchases day book posted to the purchases account. The original information for the primary records would have come from the purchase invoices.

For management information purposes it may be more useful for the purchases of each different type of raw material to be identified. Again, the information will come from the purchase invoices but instead of a single total for purchases this will be broken down into each raw material.

For all of the different costs of a business the information that is recorded in the financial accounting records will be same as that recorded in the management accounting records. The only difference will be in the way in which the information is classified and presented.

The main differences between financial accounts and management accounts can be summarised in the following table.

Financial accounts	*Management accounts*
Limited companies are required by law to prepare them	Records are not mandatory
Accordingly, the cost of record-keeping is a necessity	Accordingly, the cost of record-keeping needs to be justified
Objectives and uses are not defined by management	Objectives and uses can be laid down by management
Mainly an historical record	Regularly concerned with future results as well as historical data
Information must be compiled prudently and in accordance with legal and accounting requirements	Information should be compiled as management requires, the key criterion being relevance
Prepared for external reporting	Prepared for internal use only

3.7 COST ACCOUNTING SYSTEM

The cost accounting system is the **entire system of documentation**, accounting records and personnel that provide periodic cost accounts and cost information for management as part of the management reporting system.

3.8 BENEFITS OF COST ACCOUNTING

The main benefit is the provision of information that can be used specifically to:

- disclose profitable and unprofitable activities

- identify waste and inefficiency

- analyse movements in profit

- estimate and fix selling prices

- value inventory

- develop budgets and standards to assist planning and control

- evaluate the cost effects of policy decisions.

Thus, by a **detailed analysis** of expenditure, cost accounting becomes an important element of **managerial planning and control**.

3.9 THE TRAINEE ACCOUNTANT'S ROLE

The role of trainee accountant will depend to a large extent on the nature of the organisation they work for and the type of department they work in. In terms of a cost and management accounting system, a trainee account will typically have access to a large volume of information from the cost accounting records and will use this information to answer questions such as:

- What is the cost of a particular product, service or department?

- What is the profitability of a certain product, service or department?

- Using the cost of a product or service, what selling price should be set?

- What is the value of inventory at the end of the period?

- What is the difference between the budgeted cost and the actual cost?

4 RESPONSIBILITY CENTRES

4.1 WHAT IS A RESPONSIBILITY CENTRE?

A responsibility centre is any part of an organisation for which the performance can be measured and whose performance is the direct responsibility of a specific manager. The type of responsibility centre that is used will depend on the level of control that the individual manager is able to exercise.

4.2 COST CENTRES

Definition   A **cost centre** is a production or service location, function, activity or item of equipment for which **costs** can be determined.

A **cost centre** is a responsibility centre to which costs can be related, for example, a paint manufacturer's cost centres might be:

- mixing department

- packaging department

- stores

- maintenance

- canteen

- administration

- selling and marketing departments.

The mixing department and the packaging department are **production** cost centres as the paint is actually produced and made ready for sale in these centres. The other responsibility centres are **service** cost centres as they support the production function and provide additional services required by the organisation.

For an accountancy practice, a service organisation, the cost centres might include:

- audit
- taxation
- accountancy
- word processing
- administration
- canteen
- various geographical locations e.g. the London office, the Reading office, the Edinburgh office.

Determining the costs for each cost centre is important for:

- relating costs to cost units, i.e. to the individual units of product or service produced
- planning future costs
- controlling costs, i.e. comparing either actual to budgeted, or actual to cost to 'buy in'.

Therefore, a **cost centre manager** is responsible only for the cost incurred in the centre.

ACTIVITY 2

Try to list the cost centres in your company, or think about a company you know well and what their cost centres might be.

There is no feedback to this activity.

4.3 PROFIT CENTRES

Definition A **profit centre** is a production or service location, function or activity for which **costs and revenues, and therefore profit,** can be determined.

Thus a profit centre is a **responsibility centre** which is similar to a cost centre, but which has identifiable revenues as well as costs.

For a paint manufacturer profit centres might be a specific site or factory. For an accountancy practice the profit centres might be the individual locations or the type of business undertaken (audit, consultancy, accountancy, etc). Clearly all profit centres can also be cost centres, but not all cost centres can be profit centres.

Determining the excess of revenue over cost for each profit centre is important for:

(a) planning future profits

(b) controlling costs and revenues, i.e. comparing actual to budget

(c) measuring management performance.

The **manager of a profit centre** is therefore accountable for costs, revenues and profit.

4.4 INVESTMENT CENTRES

Definition   An **investment centre** is a production or service location, function or activity for which **costs, revenues and net assets** can be determined.

Therefore an investment centre is similar to a profit centre but as well as having identifiable costs and revenues it also has identifiable assets and liabilities.

For our paint manufacturer this could be a group of sites or factories. For the accountancy practice the Edinburgh office and the London office.

An **investment centre manager** is therefore accountable for costs, revenues, profit and assets employed in the responsibility centre. The performance of an investment centre manager can be appraised according to the level of profit achieved in relation to the value of the assets or capital employed to earn that profit. We will return in a later chapter to look at this aspect of performance measurement in more detail.

The **manager of an investment centre** is therefore accountable for costs, revenues, profit and the level of investment in the centre.

4.5 THE HIERARCHY OF RESPONSIBILITY CENTRES

Cost centres, profit centres and investment centres are often arranged in a hierarchy. There may be several cost centres within a single profit centre, several profit centres within an investment centre and several investment centres within the organisation as a whole.

5 COST UNITS

5.1 WHAT IS A COST UNIT?

A cost unit is a unit of product or service in relation to which costs are ascertained, i.e. it is the basic unit of output of the business.

For a paint manufacturer a cost unit might be a litre of paint. For an accountancy firm a cost unit might be an hour of work performed for a client.

The ascertainment of the cost per cost unit is important for:

*   making decisions about pricing
*   measuring changes in costs as the activity level changes
*   inventory valuation
*   planning future costs
*   controlling costs.

5.2 COMPOSITE COST UNITS

Composite cost units are made up of two parts and are often used in service organisations.

For example, if a hotel is monitoring its laundry costs then a possible cost unit might be a guest. However the laundry cost per guest will fluctuate depending on how many nights each guest stays. The laundry cost for a guest who stays for 14 nights would probably be more than the laundry cost of two guests who stay for only two nights each.

In this situation a more suitable cost unit for control purposes would be a cost per guest-night. Somebody who stays for 14 nights would represent 14 guest-nights and two guests who each stay for two nights would together represent four guest-nights.

Another example of the use of a composite cost unit is a transport company that monitors the cost per tonne-km, i.e. the cost of carrying one tonne for one km. The cost of carrying one tonne would not be so useful as a control measure because it would fluctuate depending on the distance travelled.

CONCLUSION

A manager is someone who is responsible for decision making, planning and control in an organisation and will require good information to carry out these tasks. By dividing the organisation into cost, profit and investment centres, responsibility for these tasks can be given to individual managers and this may motivate them to be more effective.

KEY TERMS

Data – raw facts and statistics before they have been processed.

Information – data which has been processed into a useful form.

Financial accounting – the recording and presentation of monetary transactions in accordance with statutory rules to provide the owners of the organisation with an account of the financial position at a given date.

Cost accounting – the establishment of budgets, standard costs and actual costs of operations, processes, activities or products; and the analysis of variances, profitability or the social use of funds.

Management accounting – an integral part of management concerned with identifying, presenting and interpreting information which is used for formulating strategy, planning and control, decision making and optimising the use of resources.

Cost centre – a production or service location, function, activity or item of equipment for which costs can be determined.

Profit centre – a production or service location, function or activity for which costs and revenues and therefore profits can be determined.

Investment centre – a production or service location, function or activity for which costs, revenues and net assets can be determined.

Cost unit – a unit of product or service in relation to which costs are ascertained, i.e. it is the basic unit of output of the business.

SELF TEST QUESTIONS

		Paragraph
1	Give two examples of long-term decisions that managers make.	1.2
2	What is the difference between data and information?	1.2
3	State and explain five features of effective management information.	1.5
4	What is the difference between primary data and secondary data?	2.1
5	State one source of internal and one source of external information.	2.2, 2.3
6	What do financial accounts record?	3.1
7	What is management accounting?	3.3
8	Define a cost centre, a profit centre and an investment centre.	4.2 – 4.4
9	What is a cost unit?	5.1

EXAM-STYLE QUESTIONS

1 Which of the following is not correct?

A Cost accounting can be used for inventory valuation to meet the requirements of internal reporting only.

B Management accounting provides appropriate information for decision making, planning, control and performance evaluation.

C Routine information can be used for both short-term and long-run decisions.

D Financial accounting information can be used for internal reporting purposes.

2 Which one of the following features does management information not require to be effective?

A cost effective

B sufficient accuracy

C provided immediately

D consistent.

3 Which of the following is not an example of primary data?

A An employee survey to determine views on canteen food

B A customer survey to measure product availability

C Personnel records used to assess training needs

D A Local Authority survey to assess parking needs

For suggested answers, see the 'Answers' section at the end of the book.

Chapter 3

CLASSIFICATION OF COSTS AND COST BEHAVIOUR

This chapter gives you an overview of the types of costs an organisation might incur and it also introduces you to the classification of costs. The chapter covers syllabus areas C1 (a–b)

CONTENTS

1   Classification of costs

2   Cost behaviour patterns

3   Direct costs and indirect costs

LEARNING OUTCOMES

On completion of this chapter the student should understand how to:

- Define cost classification and describe the variety of cost classifications used for different purposes in a cost accounting system, including by responsibility, function, behaviour and direct/indirect

- Describe and illustrate the nature of variable, fixed and mixed (semi-variable, stepped-fixed) costs.

1   CLASSIFICATION OF COSTS

Classification is a means of analysing costs into logical groups so that they can be summarised into meaningful information for management use or for preparing external financial reports.

Management will require information to make decisions on a variety of issues, each of which may require different cost summaries. For example costs may be required for a particular product, or for a department, or for the organisation as a whole.

The criteria used for the classification will depend on the information being collected. Some possible classifications are:

- nature – materials, labour or expenses (we will look at these in detail later on in the text)

- key responsibility or function

- product costs and period costs

- controllable costs and uncontrollable costs

- classification according to cost behaviour patterns

- direct costs and indirect costs.

1.1   FUNCTIONAL OR RESPONSIBILITY ANALYSIS OF COSTS

Costs can be analysed by **function**. This is often called analysis by **responsibility** as usually a manager will be responsible for each of these functions and their associated costs. Some possible functions within an organisation are:

Clearly the exact functions depend on the type of organisation. Organisations' activities can include:

- manufacturing products (e.g. manufacturing cars)

- providing services (such as accountants or lawyers, who do not produce a tangible 'product').

Classification of costs by function is used by management to:

- produce the financial statements

- decide which costs should or should not be included in calculations for inventory valuations

- control costs.

1.2 PRODUCT COSTS AND PERIOD COSTS

Definition **Product costs** or production costs are the costs of making, or buying, an item of inventory. For example the material and labour costs of an item are a part of its product costs.

Definition **Period costs** are those costs charged in the income statement for the period that are not directly related to the production of the goods. Period costs relate to the passage of time rather than to the output of individual products or services. Many period costs are fixed costs, which means that they are unaffected by changes in the level of activity.

Examples of period costs include most types of selling, marketing and administration costs.

This distinction between product costs and period costs is necessary to calculate inventory valuations and profit figures. We will meet this classification again when we study marginal costing and absorption costing in a later chapter.

1.3 CONTROLLABLE COSTS AND UNCONTROLLABLE COSTS

It is to be hoped that all costs that an organisation incurs are **controllable** by management at some level. However, some are **uncontrollable** as far as a particular manager is concerned.

For example, the costs of the manufacturing function of an organisation may include a centrally allocated rental cost for the factory's share of the total rent for the entire building. The factory manager will probably have **no control over the total amount of rent paid** by the organisation and may also have little or no control over the amount of floor space allocated to the factory. In this case the factory manager would view the rental cost as an uncontrollable cost. A controllable cost as far as the factory manager is concerned might be the labour cost incurred in the factory.

1.4 COST ANALYSIS BY BEHAVIOUR

Definition Analysis of costs **by behaviour** involves determining how a cost will vary if the level of activity in the organisation varies.

For example, if the level of production increased, would a particular cost increase in line with the additional output or would it remain constant and show no increase at all?

Costs can be classified by behaviour into:

- fixed costs

- variable costs

- semi-variable costs

- stepped costs.

We will study each of these classifications further in the next section of this chapter.

1.5 DIRECT COSTS AND INDIRECT COSTS

Costs can also be classified as either **direct** costs or **indirect** costs. This relates to whether the cost can be directly attributed to a particular cost centre or cost unit, in which case it is a direct cost. If a cost cannot be directly attributed to a particular cost unit or cost centre then it is classified as an indirect cost of that cost unit or cost centre.

We will return to study this classification of costs in more detail later in this chapter.

2 COST BEHAVIOUR PATTERNS

2.1 FIXED COSTS

Definition **Fixed costs** are costs that are **not affected** in total by the level of activity.

For example, the rent paid on a factory is $5,000 per month whether 2 or 200 units of output are made. This is illustrated below.

Fixed costs in total

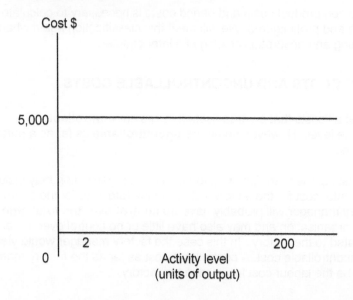

Notice that, in the short term, the amount of cost incurred on rent is $5,000 even when activity falls to zero. Notice also that the vertical axis represents the total cost incurred.

If the vertical axis represented the cost per unit the graph would be a downward sloping curve as illustrated below. This is because the same total amount of fixed cost would be shared over an increasing number of units with the result that the fixed cost per unit would fall as the level of activity increases.

Fixed cost per unit

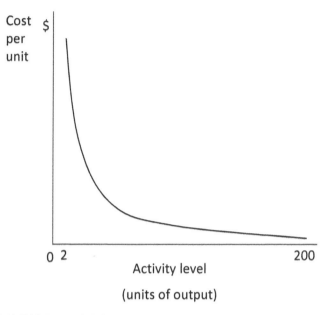

2.2 VARIABLE COSTS

Definition   **Variable costs** are costs that **change** in total in direct proportion to the level of activity.

For example if the cost of materials for a unit of output is 2 kg at $2 per kg, this amounts to $4 per unit. So, total material cost is $4 if one is made, $8 if 2 are made and $800 if 200 are made. The variable costs in total increase in line with the level of activity as shown in the diagram below.

Variable costs in total

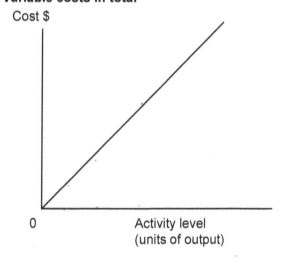

The variable cost per unit remains the same for all levels of activity i.e. $4 per unit. This can be shown on the following diagram.

Variable costs – cost per unit

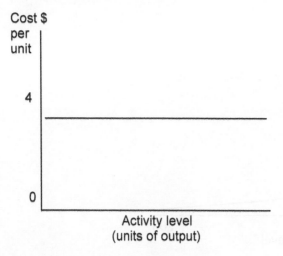

2.3 SEMI-VARIABLE COSTS

Definition **Semi-variable costs** are costs that have both a **fixed element and a variable element**.

For example a telephone bill might be a semi-variable cost. Line rental is fixed, but there is also a variable cost of calls.

Semi-variable costs are also referred to as **semi-fixed costs** or **mixed costs.**

A semi-variable cost e.g. phone bill

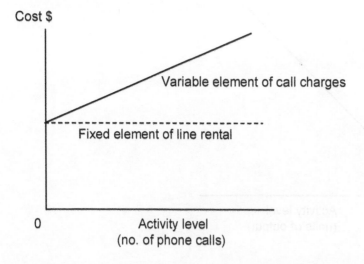

With semi-variable costs, as the level of activity increases the cost per unit falls. This can be demonstrated as follows.

If a semi-variable cost is made up of a fixed element of $2,000 and a variable element of $5 per unit, then the cost per unit will fall as the activity level rises as follows:

Activity level	100	200	300	400
Total cost	$2,500	$3,000	$3,500	$4,000
Cost per unit	$25	$15	$11.67	$10

The table above shows that the rate at which the cost per unit falls as the activity level rises is a decreasing one i.e. it falls from $25 to $15 (a $10 fall per 100 units) then from $15 to $11.67 (a fall of $3.33 per 100 units) and so on. As the volume increases, then the cost per unit will get closer and closer to simply the variable cost per unit of $5.

Semi-variable cost per unit

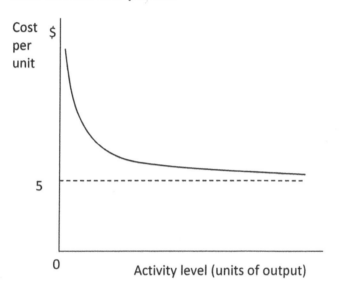

2.4 STEPPED-FIXED COSTS

Definition   **Stepped-fixed costs** are costs that are **constant for a range** of activity levels, and **then change**, and are then **constant again** for another range.

Stepped-fixed costs increase in steps as the activity level increases. For example, a factory supervisor's bonus could depend on output. At between 0 and 100 units of production, the supervisor could be paid $200, for 100 to 200 units the supervisor could be paid $300 and so on.

Stepped-fixed costs are also referred to as simply **stepped costs.**

Stepped-fixed costs e.g. supervisors' salaries

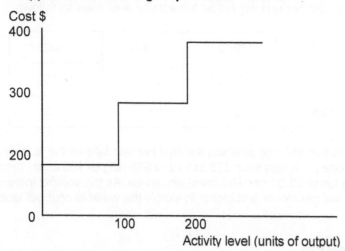

The stepped cost per unit is not constant and, as the level of activity increases within a given range of activity, the stepped cost per unit falls. This is very similar to the way in which the fixed cost per unit falls as activity levels increase. The main difference is that each time the fixed cost goes up in a 'step' the fixed cost per unit will be at its highest, and then as the level of activity increases in the given range, the stepped cost per unit will fall until the cost goes up in another 'step' again. This can be demonstrated in the table shown below for a stepped cost that increases by $5,000 as the activity levels increase by 100 units.

Activity level in units (range)	0 – 100	101 – 200	201 – 300	301 – 400
Stepped cost	$5,000	$10,000	$15,000	$20,000
Cost per unit	1 unit = $5,000	101 units = $99	201 units = $75	301 units = $66.5
	50 units = $100	150 units = $67	250 units = $60	350 units = $57
	100 units = $50	200 units = $50	300 units = $50	400 units = $50

Stepped-fixed cost per unit

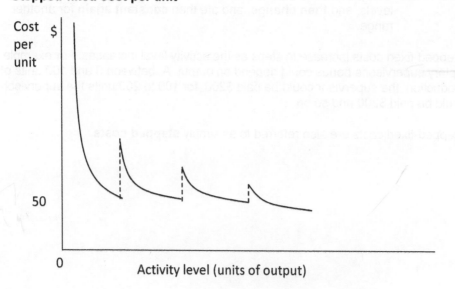

2.5   THE RELEVANT RANGE OF ACTIVITY

The cost behaviour patterns that we have described in this section will apply only for a limited range of activity. This range of activity is called the relevant range.

Definition   The **relevant range of activity** is the range of activity levels over which the observed cost behaviour patterns are valid.

For example a fixed cost will remain fixed only for a certain range of activity, after which there may be a step in the total cost incurred. It is important that managers should not attempt to use observed cost behaviour patterns to predict the cost to be incurred at activity levels that are outside the relevant range.

3   DIRECT COSTS AND INDIRECT COSTS

Definition   A **direct cost** is expenditure that can be directly identified with a specific cost unit.

Direct costs normally include the material input into the product (direct materials) the cost of the labour working on the product (direct labour) and any expenses specifically attributable to the product (direct expenses).

The total of direct costs is often referred to as the **prime cost**.

Definition   **Indirect cost** (or overhead) is expenditure that cannot be directly identified with a specific cost unit. It is jointly incurred and must be 'shared out' on an equitable basis.

Examples of indirect costs are rent and business rates.

> (**Note:** Some businesses use the term 'direct costs' in relation to cost **centres** - for example, whether costs can be directly attributable to a quality control department. However, in cost accounting - and in the exam - direct costs are those that can be allocated directly to cost **units**, as defined above. Other costs, such as the quality control costs mentioned, may be allocated directly to cost centres but they are classified as indirect costs in relation to cost units.)

3.1   TYPES OF COSTS

Every organisation will differ in terms of the precise costs that it incurs. However in general terms the main types of costs incurred by most businesses will be as follows:

- materials for the manufacture of goods

- purchases of finished goods for resale

- wages

- salaries

- other overheads.

In some service organisations, i.e. a business that provides a service rather than manufacturing a product, such as an accountancy firm, there will be very few, if any, materials costs. The majority of the costs of such a firm will be labour costs and overheads.

3.2 EXAMPLES OF DIRECT AND INDIRECT COSTS

Each type of cost will be considered in more detail in a later chapter but some examples of direct costs and indirect costs are given here:

- the **cost of the materials** directly used in the production of a product will be a **direct material cost** of the production cost centre and of the cost units produced in the cost centre

- the **cost of the oil** required for lubricating the machinery in the factory will be an **indirect cost** because it cannot be identified with specific cost units produced in the production cost centre

- the classification of **wages of the factory employees** will depend on how easy it is to identify time spent with specific units of production. For example, wages for worker handling each unit on a production line will be direct costs, whereas a supervisor's salary will be an indirect cost

- the **salary of the managing director** will be an **indirect cost** of the production cost centre as the managing director will spend only part of his time dealing with production matters

- the **repair cost** of the machinery on the factory floor will be an **indirect cost** because it cannot be identified with specific cost units produced in the cost centre

- the **electricity bill** for the organisation will be an **indirect cost** of the production cost centre – the factory uses some electricity but not all of the bill will be related to the factory and some of it will be related to other areas of the business such as the offices and canteen.

ACTIVITY 1

Murray plc has two departments – one produces cakes and the other produces tablecloths. The following expenses have been incurred this month:

1 tonne chocolate chips	$150
3 hours of a cake decorator's time	$60
Rent of the Murray plc building	$1,000
300 metres of purple cotton cloth	$2,500
2 sewing machine operators working 40 hours each	$800
Cardboard cake boxes	$40
Electricity bill for whole company	$220

Which of these costs are direct costs of production and which are indirect costs?

For a suggested answer, see the 'Answers' section at the end of the book.

3.3 ACCOUNTING FOR MATERIALS AND LABOUR

Chapter 1 included a section on accounting for materials and wages. It concluded that the double entry for the issue of materials is:

DR Work in progress control account (WIP control account)

CR Stores control account

and that the double entry for the total wage bill is:

DR Gross wages control account

CR Cost ledger control account

These double entries apply to **direct** materials and labour costs only.

The double entry for **indirect** materials or labour will debit the production overhead account.

CONCLUSION

This chapter gave you an overview of the types of costs incurred by organisations. It also looked at how the same costs can be classified in different ways according to the purpose for which management is looking at the cost. For example if management are considering increasing production of its products then classification of costs as fixed and variable would be useful. Alternatively if a comparison is being made between the performance of two similar divisions then classification into direct and indirect costs for those divisions might be most useful.

KEY TERMS

Production costs – the cost of making, or buying, an item of inventory.

Non-production, or period costs – those costs charged in the income statement for the period that are not directly related to the production of the goods.

Analysis of costs by behaviour – involves determining how a cost will vary if the level of activity in the organisation varies.

Fixed costs – costs that are not affected in total by the level of activity.

Variable costs – costs that **change** in total in direct proportion to the level of activity.

Semi-variable costs – costs that have both a fixed element and a variable element.

Stepped-fixed costs – costs that are constant for a range of activity levels, and then change, and are then constant again for another range.

Relevant range – the range of activity levels over which the observed cost behaviour patterns are valid.

Direct costs – expenditure that can be directly identified with a specific cost unit.

Indirect costs (or overheads) – expenditure that cannot be directly identified with a specific cost unit. Indirect costs are jointly incurred and must be 'shared out' on an equitable basis.

SELF TEST QUESTIONS

		Paragraph
1	What is a period cost?	1.2
2	Give an example of an uncontrollable cost.	1.3
3	Distinguish between a fixed cost and a variable cost.	2.1, 2.2
4	Would a graph of the fixed cost per unit be a straight line parallel to the horizontal axis?	2.1
5	Explain semi-variable costs.	2.3
6	What do 'direct costs' normally include?	3

EXAM-STYLE QUESTIONS

1 Which of the following statements is true of a fixed cost?

    A   increases in direct proportion to output

    B   remains constant per unit irrespective of the level of output

    C   remains constant in total irrespective of the level of output

    D   increases throughout the year.

2 Which of the costs listed below is not a variable cost?

    A   Royalties paid to the designer of a product

    B   Wages paid on an hourly basis

    C   Depreciation – based on straight-line method

    D   Materials used in production

3 Which of the following statements describes an indirect cost?

    A   a cost which cannot be influenced by its budget holder

    B   a cost which can be economically identified with a specific cost unit

    C   a cost which cannot be economically identified with a specific cost unit

    D   the highest proportion of the total cost of a product.

For suggested answers, see the 'Answers' section at the end of the book.

KAPLAN PUBLISHING

Chapter 4

CODING OF COSTS AND INCOME

This chapter looks at the use of coding in organisations, including how income and expenditure is coded. The chapter covers syllabus areas B2 (a–c) and B1(d).

CONTENTS

1　Classification and coding of costs

2　Coding of costs in practice

3　Coding income

4　Problems with coding

LEARNING OUTCOMES

On completion of this chapter the student should be able to:

- Explain and illustrate the use of codes in categorising and processing transactions.

- Explain and illustrate different methods of coding data. (including sequential, hierarchical, block, faceted and mnemonic)

- Identify and correct errors in coding of revenue and expenses.

- Describe the procedures and documentation to ensure the correct analysis and recording of sales.

1   CLASSIFICATION AND CODING OF COSTS

Cost accountants need to determine the costs that relate to each responsibility centre. To make this simpler, each expense is classified according to its responsibility centre and type of expense. A **cost code** is then allocated to the expense to represent this classification.

1.1   COST CODES

Definition   A **code** is a system of symbols designed to be applied to a classified set of items, to give a brief accurate reference, which helps entry to the records, collation and analysis.

A cost code is a code used in a costing system.

The first step in creating a cost code will be to determine the cost centre to which the cost relates and then to allocate the correct cost centre code.

Example

If a cost relates to Machine Group 7 the cost centre code might be 07. If the cost relates to the canteen the cost centre code might be 16.

1.2   GENERIC OR FUNCTIONAL CODE

Once a cost has been allocated its correct cost centre code then it may also be useful to know the particular type of expense involved. Therefore some more digits might be added to the cost centre code to represent the precise type of cost.

Example

If an expense for Machine Group 7 is for oil then its code might be 07 (for its cost centre) followed by 23 to represent indirect materials.

If an expense of the canteen is identified as frozen peas then its cost code might be 16 (its cost centre) followed by 02 to represent food purchases.

1.3   SPECIFIC CODE

Finally it may be necessary for cost allocation, decision making or accounting purposes to allocate a code which specifically identifies the item of cost.

Example

The oil for Machine Group 7 might eventually be coded as:

072304

This represents Machine Group 7 (07) indirect material use (23) of oil (04).

The frozen peas for the canteen might be coded as:

160219

This represents canteen (16) food purchases (02) of frozen peas (19).

Conclusion   A cost code is designed to analyse and classify the costs of an organisation in the most appropriate manner for that organisation. Therefore there are no set methods of designing a cost code and the cost code of a particular organisation will be that which best suits the operations and costs of that business.

ACTIVITY 1

Suppose that a cost coding system is such that the first two letters of the code represent the cost centre, the third letter the type of expense and the fourth letter the detail of the expense.

Codes are as follows:

S   Sales representative's expenses

ED   Eastern Division

P   Petrol

Write down the correct code for an Eastern Division's sales representative's petrol expenses.

For a suggested answer, see the 'Answers' section at the end of the book.

1.4   CODING SYSTEMS

There are many ways to code costs. Here are some of the more popular methods:

Sequential Code

This is the most basic type of code. It simply means that each code follows a numerical or alphabetical sequence. Planning is needed to determine how many codes might be needed in total.

For example, let's assume we are making a coding list for different types of expenses. We could give our first category, say Motor Expenses, code 001. Our next type of expense, say Electricity, would get code 002. Each expense would then follow in sequence. This allows us to have as many as 999 different types of expenses as we are using a three digit sequential code.

Block Code

Block codes are often used to categorise sequential codes together. For example, an accounting system might have the following block codes:

0000 – Expenses

1000 – Revenue

2000 – Non-current assets

3000 – Current assets

4000 – Long term liabilities

5000 – Equity

The 3000 'Block' is allocated to Current assets. This means that it is possible to classify up to 1,000 different current assets (such as different types of inventories and bank accounts) using this block.

Hierarchical Code

This text uses an hierarchical code. Each section is given a number and each sub-section is given an added decimal number. For example, codes for sales for an international electronics retailer could have the hierarchy

1   Revenue

   1.1   UK

   1.2   USA

   1.3   China

   etc.

This allows for infinite expandability. For example, A1 can be expanded as

   1.1.1   Sales of laptops within the UK

   1.1.2   Sales of photocopiers within the UK

   etc.

Each sub-category simply gets a further decimal coding.

Faceted Code

A faceted code is one that is broken down into a number of facets or fields, each of which signifies a unit of information.

Consider the following simplified table which has been extracted as a sample from the faceted code used by a large international manufacturer:

Code	Region	Code	Department	Code	Expense
01	Europe	01	Sales	0244	Salaries
02	Asia	02	Production	0245	National insurance
03	USA	03	Personnel and Finance	0246	Pension contributions
04	Africa	04	Administration	0247	Bonuses

In this example, there are three facets, or fields, to the code:

Facet 1 is the region, and is 2 digits long

Facet 2 is the department, and is 2 digits long

Facet 3 is the type of expense, and is 4 digits long

If we wanted to post an expense for a bonus paid to the production department of the USA region, the code would be:

03020247

That is: 03 (for USA), 02 (for Production) and 0247 (for Bonuses).

It can be seen that a faceted system is a complicated one and requires lots of training and possibly a table such as the one above to be used for interpretation of codes. But it does allow for more sub-divisions and a greater number of codes.

Mnemonic Code

Mnemonic means something that aids the memory or understanding. This uses an alphabetical coding rather than a numerical coding system. It is often used to abbreviate or simplify information.

For example, in accounting we might use

Code	Meaning
NCA	Non-Current Assets
EXP	Expenses
REV	Revenue

Mnemonic codes are a way of quickly expressing information and making that information easily understood. However, this coding method makes it very difficult to use sub-categories or to have too much information. Mnemonic coding is likely to struggle to categorise 999 different types of expenses, for example.

1.5 PURPOSES OF COST CODES

The main purposes of cost codes are to:

- **assist precise information**: costs incurred can be associated with pre-established codes, so reducing variations in classification
- **facilitate electronic data processing**: computer analysis, summarisation and presentation of data can be performed more easily through the use of codes
- **facilitate a logical and systematic arrangement of costing records**: accounts can be arranged in blocks of codes permitting additional codes to be inserted in logical order
- **simplify comparison of totals of similar expenses** rather than all of the individual items
- **incorporate check codes** within the main code to check the accuracy of the postings.

Example

Owen Ltd manufactures motorbike helmets.

It has four sales areas and two factories that are coded as:

Scotland and the North	100
Midlands	101
South East	102
South West	103

Factories:

Slough	110
Leeds	111

Cost centres:

Machining	120
Finishing	121
Packing	122
Stores	123
Canteen	124
Maintenance	125
Administration	126

Type of expense:

Direct labour	200
Direct material	201
Direct expenses	202
Indirect labour	203
Indirect material	204
Indirect expenses (overheads)	205
Sales revenue:	210

Thus, the cost of direct labour in the Finishing Department at the Leeds factory would be coded 111/121/200.

ACTIVITY 2

The following is a list of costs and revenues relating to a business activity. Code these using the structure above:

(i)   Slough factory, cleaning materials used in the canteen

(ii)   Slough factory, wages for stores personnel

(iii) Leeds factory, metered power (electricity) for Machining Department

(iv)   Leeds factory, telephone account for site as a whole

(v)   Sales from Slough factory to customer in Exeter

(vi)   Slough factory, general maintenance material for repairs.

For a suggested answer, see the 'Answers' section at the end of the book.

2   CODING OF COSTS IN PRACTICE

2.1   TIMING OF CODING

In order to be of most use the coding of costs should take place when the cost or expense is first received by the organisation. In most cases this will be when the invoice for the goods is received.

After this point the documents will be entered into the accounting system and then to the filing system so it is important that the coding is done immediately.

2.2   RECEIVING AN INVOICE

When an invoice is received by the organisation it will undergo a variety of checks to ensure that it is for valid purchases that were ordered and have been received or that it is for a service that has been received. In the process of these checks it will become clear what type of goods or service is being dealt with, for example it may be an invoice for the purchase of raw materials for the factory or an electricity bill for the entire organisation.

Once the invoice has been checked for validity then it must be correctly coded.

2.3   CHOOSING THE CORRECT CODE

In order for the correct code to be given to the invoice, it is vital that the person responsible for the coding fully understands the nature of the organisation and the costs that it incurs. The organisation's coding listing should be referred to and the correct cost centre, type and expense code should be entered on the front of the invoice.

2.4   INDIRECT COSTS

Some costs, for example electricity bills, cannot be allocated directly to a single cost centre as they are indirect costs. Eventually a portion of this electricity bill will be shared out to each of the cost centres that uses electricity but at the point where the account is being coded it must simply be recognised that this is an indirect cost and should be coded to an overhead cost centre.

Therefore, the coding structure of the organisation should include some codes that specifically identify a cost as an indirect cost.

2.5   CHEQUE AND CASH PAYMENTS

As well as receiving invoices for costs incurred on credit most organisations will also write cheques for costs and even pay some costs out of petty cash. These costs must be coded in just the same way as expenses on credit.

If the payment is by cheque then there will be some documentation to support that payment. When this documentation is authorised for payment then it should also be coded for costing purposes.

If payments are made out of petty cash then they must be supported by a petty cash voucher. Again this voucher must be coded according to the type of cost.

Example of a coded petty cash voucher

Petty Cash Voucher	No. _340_		
Date _22/3/X3_			
For what required		AMOUNT $	c
Stamps Code 111/121/200		7	10
Signature _P Nelson_			
Authorised _John Falk_			

2.6 PAYMENT OF WAGES AND SALARIES

Wages and salaries normally form a very large part of the costs incurred by an organisation. If wages or salaries are paid by cheque or in cash then the supporting documentation, the payslip, or the summary of all labour costs, the payroll, should be coded as with other cash payments. However wages and salaries are often paid directly into employees' bank accounts through the BACS system. Therefore it is important that the wages and salaries costs are coded according to the department or cost centre so that the total direct and indirect labour cost of the cost centre is known.

3 CODING INCOME

If an organisation has profit or investment centres then the income of the organisation must also be correctly coded.

3.1 SALES INVOICES

If an organisation makes sales on credit then when the sales invoice is raised it should be coded according to the coding listing. This code will probably specify the profit centre or investment centre that has made the sale and often also the product or service that is being sold.

3.2 CASH SALES

In a retail organisation sales may be made for cash. There should always be documentation that supports the cash takings, such as the till rolls for the day. This documentation needs to be coded to reflect the profit or investment centre that made the sales and any other detailed product coding that is required by the organisation. Most modern cash registers will automatically code each sale, using Electronic Point of Sale (EPOS) devices which include bar code readers.

4 PROBLEMS WITH CODING

4.1 WHICH CODE?

The main problem when coding documents is deciding which cost centre and analysis code to use; the documents may not clearly show which cost centre incurred the costs or what type of cost it is.

If you are unable to code a document try the following:

- looking in the organisation's procedures book or policy manual

- referring the query document to your supervisor.

4.2 APPORTIONMENT

If more than one cost centre has incurred the cost (for example, a heating bill for the whole building), the cost needs to be shared between all of the cost centres (or **apportioned**). Although it may be easy to simply share the costs equally between the cost centres, some cost centres may be bigger than others and therefore use more electricity/heating, etc. – so should receive a greater percentage of the cost. You should refer to your organisation's procedures book or policy manual or ask your supervisor for advice when coding costs like this.

4.3 OTHER CODING PROBLEMS

You may come across other coding problems, such as:

- The wrong code used: this would mean that the information on the accounting system is also wrong. Codes need to be very carefully checked.

- The wrong organisation: occasionally, an invoice might arrive that is for a company with a similar name or address. You should check invoice details carefully so that errors like this are not entered on to the accounting system.

4.4 IDENTIFYING AND CORRECTING ERRORS

Errors in coding are usually detected via the internal controls of the company or through the activities of internal and external auditors. For example,

- Reconciling a suppliers outstanding balance between the purchase ledger and the supplier's statement may reveal differences in invoices (too many or some missing). The discrepancy may be due to the miss-coding of these invoices which can then be rechecked

- Some businesses have built in logic checks into the way items are coded. Any anomalies would be shown in an exceptions report.

- Internal auditors may check a sample of invoices to ensure they are correctly coded.

Correction of errors involves

- reversing out the accounting entries for the original incorrect coding

- correctly coding the item and reposting the accounting entries.

CONCLUSION

You should now know why it is important to code costs and income. If actual costs and income are to be used for management purposes then it is vital that they are correctly classified and coded to ensure that they are allocated to the correct cost, profit or investment centre. Only then can any useful management information be obtained.

KEY TERM

Code – a system of symbols designed to be applied to a classified set of items, to give a brief accurate reference, which helps entry to the records, collation and analysis.

SELF TEST QUESTIONS

		Paragraph
1	Define the term 'cost code'.	1.1
2	List three purposes of cost codes.	1.4
3	How are costs coded in practice?	2

EXAM-STYLE QUESTIONS

1   A company operates from three main sites. In analysing its overhead costs it uses a nine-digit coding system. A sample from the coding manual shows:

Site		Expenditure type		Function	
Whitby	100	Rent	410	Purchasing	600
Scarborough	200	Power	420	Finance	610
York	300	Heat and light	430	Production	620
		Travel costs	500	Sales	630
		Telephone and postage	520		

The order of coding is: site/expense/function

How would an invoice for the York site for travel costs incurred by a sales representative be coded?

A   300/500/600

B   300/500/630

C   300/500/610

D   300/500/620

2   G plc has a coding system where the code for 'non-current assets' starts with the letters 'NCA'

What type of coding system is G plc using?

A   Sequential

B   Mnemonic

C   Hierarchical

D   Faceted

3   How should an indirect selling cost be coded?

A   It should be coded to a cost unit

B   It should be coded to finished goods

C   It should be coded to an overhead cost centre

D   It should not be coded at all.

For suggested answers, see the 'Answers' section at the end of the book.

Chapter 5

MATERIALS COST

It is important to be able to distinguish between direct material and indirect material costs in order to determine product cost. This chapter looks at the distinction between such costs and the physical and financial control of these materials. The chapter covers syllabus areas B1(a and b), C1(c), D1(a, b and c).

CONTENTS

1   Materials cost classification

2   Stores department

3   Materials control cycle

4   Recording materials costs

5   Pricing issues of materials

6   Bookkeeping entries

7   Controlling inventory levels

LEARNING OUTCOMES

On completion of this chapter the student should be able to:

- Describe the material control cycle (including the concept of 'free' inventory, but excluding control levels and EOQ) and the documentation necessary to order, receive, store and issue materials.

- Describe the procedures and documentation to ensure the correct authorisation, analysis and recording of direct and indirect material costs.

- Describe and illustrate the classification of material costs.

- Distinguish different types of material (raw material, work in progress and finished goods).

- Describe and illustrate the accounting for material costs.

- Explain and illustrate different methods used to price materials issued from inventory (FIFO, LIFO and periodic and cumulative weighted average costs).

---

1 MATERIALS COST CLASSIFICATION

The main classifications for materials used by the management accountant are direct materials and indirect materials.

1.1 TYPES OF INVENTORY

For a retailer the main type of inventory will be goods bought for resale.

For a manufacturer, however, we can identify three types of inventory:

- raw materials
- work in progress (WIP)
- finished goods

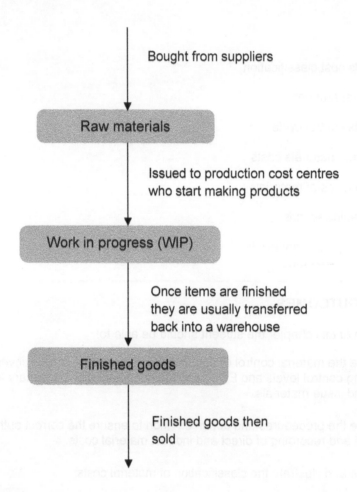

1.2 MATERIALS

For manufacturers various materials are needed to make the main product of the business.

Remember that, for management accounting purposes, costs can be classified as either direct or indirect. Materials are no exception to this.

1.3   DIRECT MATERIALS

Definition   **Direct materials** are the materials that can be economically attributed to a specific unit of production.

The direct materials are therefore the raw materials that are directly input into the products that an organisation makes. For example, the metal used to make spoons or the flour to make bread.

1.4   INDIRECT MATERIALS

Definition   **Indirect materials** are other materials used in the production process that cannot be directly attributed to a unit of production.

An example of indirect materials might be the oil used for the lubrication of production machinery. This is a material that is used in the production process but it cannot be directly attributed to each unit of finished product.

1.5   DIRECT MATERIAL ITEMS CLASSIFIED AS INDIRECT COSTS

Notice that the definition of direct materials included the word 'economically'. On occasions certain costs may be incurred which are strictly direct material costs but for which it would not be economical to classify as such.

For example direct material items which have a low unit cost and are used in large volumes may be classified as indirect costs because it is not worth the effort of classifying them as direct and tracing the cost to individual units. Examples include staples, nails, screws and so on.

The benefit of the greater 'accuracy' from treating such items as direct material is not worth the cost and administrative effort.

1.6   WORK IN PROGRESS

Work in progress (WIP) refers to units that have been started but are incomplete at the end of the accounting period.

For example a wooden table may have had the top made but is still waiting for legs to be attached.

1.7   FINISHED GOODS

Finished goods are completed and ready for selling to customers.

2   STORES DEPARTMENT

2.1   FUNCTION OF THE STORES DEPARTMENT

The stores department is responsible for the receipt, storage, issue and recording of the raw materials used in the production process.

2.2 RECEIPT OF GOODS

When raw materials are received from suppliers they will normally be delivered to the stores department.

The stores personnel must check the original purchase order to ensure that the goods delivered are the ones that have been ordered, in the correct quantity, of the correct quality and in good condition.

2.3 STORAGE OF MATERIALS

Once the materials have been received they must be stored until required by the production departments.

Storage of materials must be appropriate to their type. For example foodstuffs must be stored at the correct temperature and wood must be stored in dry conditions. Storage should also be laid out in such a manner that the correct materials can be accessed easily either manually or by machinery.

2.4 ISSUE OF MATERIALS

When the production departments require raw materials for production it is essential that the stores department can provide the correct quantity and quality of materials at the time they are required. This will require careful attention to inventory control policies to ensure that the most efficient levels of raw materials inventory are kept.

2.5 RECORDING OF RECEIPTS AND ISSUES

In many organisations the stores department is also responsible for the recording of the quantities of raw materials that are received from suppliers and issued to the production departments. This normally takes place on the **bin cards** (see section 4.1).

3 MATERIALS CONTROL CYCLE

3.1 INTRODUCTION

Materials can often form the largest single item of cost for a business so it is essential that the material purchased is the most suitable for the intended purpose.

3.2 CONTROL OF PURCHASING

When goods are purchased they must be ordered, received by the stores department, recorded, issued to the manufacturing department that requires them and eventually paid for. This process needs a great deal of paperwork and strict internal controls.

Internal control consists of full documentation and appropriate authorisation of all transactions in and movements of materials and authorisation of all requisitions, orders, receipts and payments.

If control is to be maintained over purchasing, it is necessary to ensure that:

- only necessary items are purchased

- orders are placed with the most appropriate supplier after considering price and delivery details

- the goods that are actually received are the goods that were ordered and in the correct quantity

- the price paid for the goods is correct (i.e. what was agreed when the order was placed).

To ensure that all of this takes place requires a reliable system of checking and control.

3.3 OVERVIEW OF PROCEDURES

It is useful to have an overview of the purchasing process.

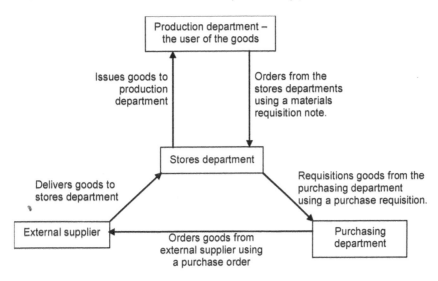

There are many variations of the above system in practice, but it is a fairly typical system and does provide good control over the purchasing and issuing process.

ACTIVITY 1

Your organisation may have a slightly different process to this. See if you can draw a similar diagram illustrating the way your organisation's (or a familiar organisation's) purchasing process works.

There is no feedback to this activity.

3.4 PURCHASE REQUISITION

It is important that an organisation controls the goods that are ordered from suppliers. Only goods that are genuinely necessary should be ordered. Therefore, before any order for goods is placed, a purchase requisition must be completed.

Each purchase requisition must be authorised by the appropriate person. This will usually be the storekeeper or store manager.

When the purchase requisition has been completed it is sent to the purchasing department so that the purchase order is prepared.

3.5 PURCHASE ORDER

Purchase orders will be placed with suppliers by the purchasing department. The choice of supplier will depend upon the price, delivery promise, quality of goods and past performance.

The person placing the order must first check that the purchase requisition has been authorised by the appropriate person in the organisation.

Once the supplier of the goods has been chosen, the purchase price of the goods must be determined.

This will either be from the price list of the supplier or from a special quotation of the price by that supplier. The price agreed will be entered on the purchase order together with details of the goods being ordered.

The purchase order must then be authorised by the appropriate person in the organisation before it is dispatched to the supplier.

A copy of the purchase order is sent to the goods receiving department or stores department as confirmation of expected delivery. The goods receiving department therefore know that goods are due and can alert appropriate management if they are not received. A copy is also sent to the accounts department to be matched to the supplier's invoice. An example purchase order is show below.

BLACKHILL FILES
742 St Anne's Way
York YO5 4NP
Telephone: 01904 27635
Registered in England, No 1457893

PURCHASE ORDER

Printing Unlimited   Order No: 35762
80 New High Street
Exeter   Ref: T.Holmes
EX4 2LP

Date: 22 June 20X4

Please print 25,000 labels at $10.50 from copy supplied per 1,000

Needed by 20 July 20X4

Payment within 30 days of delivery. 2% early settlement discount

Delivery to: As above

3.6 DELIVERY NOTE

A delivery note is sent by the supplier with the goods being delivered. This must include full details of the goods being delivered. The delivery note is signed by the person receiving the goods as evidence that the goods arrived.

3.7 GOODS RECEIVED NOTE

When goods are received by the organisation they will usually be taken to a central goods receiving department or stores department rather than being delivered directly to the part of the organisation that will use the goods. This enables the receipt of goods to be controlled.

The goods receiving department or stores department have copies of all purchase orders. It is important that the goods that arrive actually agree in **all** detail to those ordered before they are accepted.

When the goods are received, the stores department will firstly check what the goods are. They will be identified and counted and the supplier and purchase order to which they relate will be identified.

The details of the delivery note are checked to the actual goods and to the purchase order. It is important that the stores department checks that these goods were actually ordered by the organisation before accepting them.

Finally, when the stores department is satisfied with all of the details of the delivery, the details are recorded on a goods received note (GRN).

Any concerns about the goods being delivered (for example, too few, too many, the wrong colour, the wrong size) should be referred immediately to the appropriate manager before accepting the goods.

The GRN is evidence that the goods that were ordered have been received and therefore should be, and can be, paid for. The GRN will, therefore, be sent to the accounts department to be matched with the supplier's invoice.

As evidence of the actual receipt of the goods the GRN is also used for entering receipts of materials in the stores records.

3.8 PURCHASE INVOICE

The purchase invoice for goods details the amount that the receiver of the goods must pay for them and the date that payment is due. The purchase invoice might be included when the goods themselves are delivered, or might be sent after delivery.

The person responsible for payment must check that the details of the purchase invoice agree to the goods received note, the delivery note and the purchase order. This is to ensure that:

- what was ordered was received

- what was received is what is being paid for

- the price charged is that agreed.

Once it is certain that the purchase invoice agrees with the goods that were actually received then the invoice can be authorised for payment by the appropriate person in the organisation.

4 RECORDING MATERIALS COSTS

4.1 BIN CARDS

The storekeeper must know at any time the level of inventory of any item. This is done by use of a bin card.

Definition A **bin card** is a simple record of receipts, issues and inventory balances in hand kept by storekeepers, recorded in quantities of materials.

The bin card is a duplication of the quantity information recorded in the stores ledger (see later in this chapter) but storekeepers frequently find that such a ready record is a very useful aid in carrying out their duties.

An example of a bin card for an item of inventory is given as follows:

BIN CARD

Description ....Chipboard.... Location ....Stores.... Code ..D35..

Maximum ..3,000m.. Minimum ..1,000m.. Reorder level ..1,400m.. Reorder quantity 200m

Receipts			Issues			Current inventory level	On order		
Date	GRN Ref	Quantity	Date	Issue Ref	Quantity		Date	Ref	Quantity
30/7/X3	8737	200m				200m	01/8/X3	PO6752	300m
06/8/X3	8748	300m				500m			
			07/8/X9	3771	400m				

The bin card does not have value columns.

4.2 MATERIALS REQUISITION NOTE

Materials issued to production departments from the stores department are controlled by a materials requisition note (also referred to as a stores requisition or goods requisition note). This document authorises the storekeeper to release the goods.

4.3 MATERIALS RETURNED NOTE

When unused materials are returned from user departments to the stores, the transaction will be recorded on a document similar to the materials requisition but usually printed in a different colour. This will be a materials returned note or goods returned note. It will be completed by the user department that is returning the goods and signed by the storekeeper as evidence that the goods were returned to stores.

These returns must also be recorded in the bin card and material inventory account.

When the goods are returned the details on the goods returned note must be checked to the actual goods themselves.

4.4   SUMMARY OF DOCUMENTS USED

Purchase requisition:

- filled out by stores
- authorised
- sent to purchasing department.

Purchase order:

- filled out by purchasing department
- supplier chosen by purchasing department
- price of goods calculated from price list
- authorised
- sent to supplier.

Delivery note:

- provided by supplier with delivery
- received together with goods by stores department
- compared to actual goods
- goods checked and counted
- delivery note and goods checked to purchase order.

Goods received note:

- a document produced by stores department for their own use
- goods checked and counted
- written up and signed
- matched with delivery note and purchase order
- sent to accounts to await purchase invoice.

Purchase invoice:

- received from supplier
- checked to purchase order, delivery note and goods received note
- authorised for payment
- payment made.

Materials requisition note:

- filled out by user department
- authorised
- sent to stores.

Materials returned note:

- filled out by returning department
- actual goods checked against goods returned note by stores
- signed as evidence of receipt.

Bin card:

- maintained by stores department

- written up from goods received note, materials requisition note and goods returned note

- shows quantity of goods held in stores.

4.5 STORES CONTROL ACCOUNT

The accounting for material is dealt with through a **stores control account** (or a **materials inventory account**). This is maintained by the accounting department and the physical inventory shown on these accounts is reconciled with the bin card.

Definition A **stores control account** records the quantity and value of receipts, issues and the current balance of each item of inventory. This would cover both direct and indirect material held in inventory.

Example

Vibrant Ltd has recently placed an order for 5,000 adhesive strips, showing the company logo, which are used on the company's range of products. It currently has 100 units in inventory at a value of $25. The invoice from the supplier, Slough Labels Ltd shows:

Slough Labels Ltd 3 Station Unit Slough SL1 3EJ		Vat No:	724371692
		Tax point	31 June X4
Tel: 01947 825431 Fax: 01947 825429 email: Sloughlab@virgin.net		Invoice No:	**72936**

INVOICE			
To: Vibrant Ltd 10 Royal Crescent Whitby YO21 3EA		Order No:	7921

Qty	Description	Unit price	Value $
5,000	Ad Label TS 12	$0.25 each	1,250.00
	Sales Tax 17½%		218.75
			$1,468.75
Terms:	Net 30 days		

Note:

This purchase invoice might be coded as:

110	/	121	/	201	$1,250.00
Slough		Finishing		Direct	
Factory		cost centre		material	

The Sales Tax would be coded separately.

The Goods Received Note would be completed on receipt of the goods:

VIBRANT LTD			
GOODS RECEIVED NOTE			**No: GRN 272**
SUPPLIER: Slough Labels		DATE: PURCHASE ORDER NO:	25/6/X4 TS 7921

DESCRIPTION	CODE	QTY	NO OF PACKAGES
AD Labels	TS 12	5,000	1

Received by: STORES – FINISHING AREA

Required by: FINISHING COST CENTRE 121

Accepted by: STORES SUPERVISOR

QUALITY ASSURANCE *J. Smith*

Inspected by: SIG: ....

Qty passed: 5,000 **Qty rejected:** Nil

The materials inventory card would be completed as follows:

INVENTORY LEDGER ACCOUNT

AD LABELS

Material .... Maximum quantity ....

Code ......TS 12.. .... Minimum quantity ....

Receipts					Issues					Balance		
Date	GRN No	Qty	Price $	Amount $	Date	Material requisition	Qty	Price	Amount	Qty	Price $	Value $
										100	0.25	25.00
25/6	272	5,000	0.25	1,250.00						5,100	0.25	1,275.00

Similarly, if inventory is issued for use then entries would be made in the issues columns of the materials inventory card and the balances of inventory held reduced. Periodic inventory checks will be made to ensure the physical inventory held is in accordance with the bin card (and therefore the materials inventory cards) and any discrepancies should be investigated.

4.6 CODING

In order to ensure that the correct amount of materials cost is recorded against a cost centre all movements of materials need to be coded and described as appropriate throughout the recording process.

5 PRICING ISSUES OF MATERIALS

When materials are purchased, the process of giving them a value is fairly straightforward. The purchase cost of the items is the price charged by the supplier (excluding any Sales Tax) plus any carriage inwards costs. The cost should be net of any trade discount given.

> When materials are issued from store, a cost or price has to be attached to them.

- When a quantity of materials is purchased in its entirety for a specific job, the purchase cost can be charged directly to the job.

- More commonly however, materials are held in inventory and replaced when used. Consequently, when issues of materials from store are being valued/priced, we do not try to identify what the specific units actually did cost. Instead, materials issued from store are valued/priced on the basis of a valuation method.

A business might use any of several valuation methods for pricing stores issued. Three such methods are:

- First in first out (FIFO)

- Last in first out (LIFO)

- Weighted average cost (AVCO).

EXAMPLE

The same example will be used to illustrate each of these methods.

In November 1,000 tonnes of inventory item 1234 were purchased in three lots:

3 November	400 tonnes at $60 per tonne
11 November	300 tonnes at $70 per tonne
21 November	300 tonnes at $80 per tonne

During the same period four materials requisitions were completed for 200 tonnes each, on 5, 14, 22 and 27 November.

5.1 FIRST IN FIRST OUT (FIFO) METHOD

With the first in first out method of valuation, it is assumed that materials are issued from store in the order in which they were received. In the example above, it would be assumed with FIFO that the 400 tonnes purchased at $60 each on 3 November will be used before the 300 tonnes bought on 11 November, and these in turn will be used before the 300 tonnes bought on 21 November.

The closing inventory at the end of November is 200 units. These consist of 200 of the most recently purchased units.

The stores ledger account for inventory item 1234 is summarised below.

Date	Receipts	Issues	Balance No.	$
3 Nov	400 × $60		400	24,000
5 Nov		200 × $60	200	12,000
11 Nov	300 × $70		500	33,000
14 Nov		200 × $60	300	21,000
21 Nov	300 × $80		600	45,000
22 Nov		200 × $70	400	31,000
27 Nov		100 × $70		
		100 × $80	200	16,000

Note that each successive consignment into stores is exhausted before charging issues from stores at the next price.

Using this method the total value of materials issued is $53,000 and the value of closing inventory is $16,000.

5.2 LAST IN FIRST OUT (LIFO) METHOD

With the last in first out method of pricing, it is assumed that materials issued from stores are the units that were acquired the most recently of those still remaining in inventory.

In this example, the 200 tonnes issued on 5 November will therefore consist of materials purchased on 3 November, the 200 tonnes issued on 14 November will consist of materials purchased on 11 November and the 200 tonnes issued on 22 November will consist of materials purchased on 21 November. The materials issued on 27 November will consist of the remaining 100 tonnes bought on 21 November and the 100 tonnes bought on 14 November.

The closing inventory at the end of November consists of 200 of the tonnes bought on 3 November.

The stores ledger card for item 1234 using LIFO would be as follows.

Date	Receipts	Issues	Balance No.	$
3 Nov	400 × $60		400	24,000
5 Nov		200 × $60	200	12,000
11 Nov	300 × $70		500	33,000
14 Nov		200 × $70	300	19,000
21 Nov	300 × $80		600	43,000
22 Nov		200 × $80	400	27,000
27 Nov		100 × $80		
		100 × $70	200	12,000

Using this method the total value of materials issued is $57,000 (more than under FIFO) and the closing inventory value is $12,000 (less than FIFO). When prices are rising this will always be the case.

5.3 CUMULATIVE WEIGHTED AVERAGE COST (AVCO) METHOD

With the cumulative weighted average cost method of pricing material issues, all quantities of an item of inventory are valued at a weighted average cost. A new weighted average cost is calculated each time that there is a new delivery into stores. A weighted average price is usually calculated to the nearest cent.

Weighted average price = $\dfrac{\text{Inventory value of items in stores} + \text{Purchase cost of units received}}{\text{Quantity already in stores} + \text{Quantity received}}$

The price so calculated is used to value all subsequent issues until the next consignment of the inventory is received into stores and a new weighted average cost is calculated.

	Item 1234			
	Receipts (issues)			Weighted average price
Date	Quantity	Purchase price	Value	(issue price)
		$	$	$
3 Nov	400	60	24,000	60
5 Nov	(200)		(12,000)	60
	200		12,000	60
11 Nov	300	70	21,000	
Balance	500		33,000	66 (W1)
14 Nov	(200)		(13,200)	66
	300		19,800	66
21 Nov	300	80	24,000	
Balance	600		43,800	73 (W2)
22 Nov	(200)		(14,600)	73
27 Nov	(200)		(14,600)	73
30 Nov (bal)	200		14,600	73

A new average cost price calculation is required after each new receipt.

Workings

(W1) $33,000/500 = $66

(W2) $43,800/600 = $73

Using this method the total value of materials issued is $54,400 and the closing inventory value is $14,600. These figures are between the FIFO and LIFO valuations.

The above method looks at the AVCO on a continuous **cumulative** basis. A variation on the AVCO method is the **periodic** weighted average cost method.

5.4 PERIODIC WEIGHTED AVERAGE COST METHOD

With the periodic weighted average cost method of pricing inventory an average price is calculated at the end of the period which is then used to price all issues.

Periodic weighted average price =

$$\frac{\text{Cost of opening inventory} + \text{Cost of all receipts in the period}}{\text{Units in opening inventory} + \text{Units received}}$$

The stores ledger card for the item 1234 would be as follows: Item 1234

Date	Quantity	Purchase price	Value	Periodic Weighted Average price (issue price)
		Receipts (Issues)		
3 Nov	400	60	24,000	
11 Nov	300	70	21,000	
21 Nov	300	80	24,000	
	1,000		69,000	69.00
5 Nov	(200)		(13,800)	69.00
14 Nov	(200)		(13,800)	69.00
22 Nov	(200)		(13,800)	69.00
27 Nov	(200)		(13,800)	69.00
30 Nov (bal)	200		13,800	69.00

Using this method the total value of materials issued is $55,200 and the closing inventory value is $13,800. Note that using this method the cost of issues cannot be calculated until the end of the period.

ACTIVITY 2

You are given the following information about one line of inventory held by Tolley plc.

Assuming that there are no further transactions in the month of May, what is the value of the issues made on 1 March and 1 May and what would be the inventory valuation, using (i) the FIFO valuation method (ii) LIFO and (iii) AVCO (iv) Periodic weighted average pricing?

How does the inventory pricing method used impact on the profit made on sales?

		Units	Cost $	Sales price $
Opening inventory	1 January	50	7	
Purchase	1 February	60	8	
Sale	1 March	40		10
Purchase	1 April	70	9	
Sale	1 May	60		12

For a suggested answer, see the 'Answers' section at the end of the book.

6 BOOKKEEPING ENTRIES

6.1 ACCOUNTING FOR MATERIALS COSTS

In a cost accounting system, **transactions involving materials costs** are recorded in a **stores control account**. These transactions are mainly the purchase of stores items and the issue of materials to various departments within the organisation. The stores account also records the value of opening inventory and closing inventory of materials at the beginning and end of each period. Inventory may be raw materials in a manufacturing environment or material inputs in a service environment.

Depending on the nature and use of the materials the issues made from stores could go to any of the following:

- The **work-in-progress account**, which records the costs of items manufactured. The account records costs in total, but the costs might be broken down into the costs of individual jobs or processes or the costs of individual products. The opening balance and closing balance on this account at the start and end of a period represent the total cost of unfinished production. The cost of WIP will include raw materials, labour and overheads.

- The **production overhead account**, which records indirect production costs, including indirect production materials.

- Other accounts, including selling and admin overheads

Example

A company has the following information

Opening balances of:		
	Raw materials	$2,000
	Work-in-progress	$1,500
	Finished goods	$8,000

Transactions recorded in the period	
Material purchases	$40,000
Direct materials issued to production	$21,000
Indirect materials issued to production	$3,000
Indirect materials issued to administration	$6,000
Indirect materials issued to selling	$5,000

This information can be used to prepare the stores control account.

Stores control account

	$		$
Opening inventory	2,000	Work-in-progress	21,000
Creditors account	40,000	*(Direct materials issued to production)*	
(Material purchases)			
		Production overheads	3,000
		Admin overheads	6,000
		Selling/dist'n overheads	5,000
		(Indirect materials consumed)	
		Closing inventory *(Balancing figure)*	7,000
	———		———
	42,000		42,000
	———		———

7 CONTROLLING INVENTORY LEVELS

7.1 INTRODUCTION

It is the responsibility of the storekeeper to ensure that inventory is held at the optimum level. If inventory levels are too high then unnecessary costs associated with storage will be incurred. In addition, insurance costs will increase and there will also be a cost attached to the capital tied up in holding inventory. On the other hand, if inventory levels are too low then there is a risk of running out of inventory with consequent disruptions to the production process, the loss of sales to customers (and hence loss of customer goodwill) and possibly high costs incurred to obtain emergency supplies.

7.2 FREE INVENTORY

An important control level that the storekeeper might use when monitoring the level of inventory is called the free inventory (or free stock).

Definition **Free inventory** is the inventory that is in stores or on order from a supplier which has not yet been requisitioned for a specific use.

Free inventory is calculated as follows:

Free inventory = Inventory in stores + Inventory on order from suppliers – Inventory already requisitioned for use

Example

There are 457 units of item 982 in inventory. The stores department has outstanding materials requisitions from production cost centres amounting to 280 units in total. An order for 400 units has been placed with the supplier and delivery is expected in three days.

What is the free inventory of item 982?

Solution

Free inventory = 457 units in inventory + 400 units on order – 280 units requisitioned

= 577 units

By monitoring the level of free inventory the storekeeper attempts to ensure that inventory is maintained at the optimum level.

7.3 RAW MATERIAL REQUIREMENTS

The raw materials required to be purchased in a period can be determined as follows:

Budgeted raw materials purchases = Budgeted raw materials usage *plus* Budgeted closing inventory of raw materials *less* Budgeted opening inventory of raw materials.

Example – calculating material requirements

Budgeted sales of product C for next period are 4,500 units. Each unit of product C requires 4 kg of raw material.

Details of budgeted inventory requirements are as follows:

	Opening inventory	Closing inventory
Raw materials	4,200 kg	4,600 kg
Product C	1,100 units	800 units

Solution

Production budget – product C

	Units
Sales requirement	4,500
Closing inventory	800
	5,300
Opening inventory	1,100
Budgeted production	4,200

Raw materials purchases budget

	Kg
Production requirements (4,200 × 4 kg)	16,800
Closing inventory	4,600
	21,400
Opening inventory	4,200
Budgeted purchases	17,200

CONCLUSION

Organisations for which material is a major cost should have well-defined procedures for ordering, receiving and accounting for inventory. This will include allocating appropriate authority to managers and the careful control of inventory.

KEY TERMS

Direct materials – the materials that can be economically attributed to a specific unit of production.

Indirect materials – other materials used in the production process that cannot be directly attributed to a unit of production.

Bin card – a simple record of receipts, issues and balances of inventory in hand kept by storekeepers, recorded in quantities of materials.

Materials inventory account – records the quantity and value of receipts, issues and the current balance of each item of inventory. This would cover both direct and indirect material held in inventory.

Free inventory – inventory that is in stores or on order from a supplier which has not yet been requisitioned for a specific use.

FIFO – first in first out method of inventory valuation.

LIFO – last in first out method of inventory valuation.

AVCO – weighted average method of inventory valuation.

SELF TEST QUESTIONS

		Paragraph
1	Give three examples of both direct and indirect material costs.	1.1, 1.2
2	What is the purpose of a purchase requisition?	3.4
3	Which department issues a materials requisition note?	4.2
4	What information is recorded in a materials inventory account?	4.5
5	What is meant by free inventory?	5.2

EXAM-STYLE QUESTIONS

1   When charging a direct materials cost to a cost centre, the details would be taken from which document?

   A   Purchase requisition

   B   Material requisition

   C   Goods received note

   D   Purchase order

2   Which of the following are least likely to be classified as a direct material cost?

   A   Flour for a baker

   B   Material for a dressmaker

   C   Plants for a landscape gardener

   D   Glue for a toy maker

3   Who is usually responsible for authorising the purchase requisition?

   A   Purchasing manager

   B   Stores manager

   C   Production manager

   D   Management accountant.

The following information relates to questions 4 – 6

ABC Ltd had an opening inventory of $880 (275 units valued at $3.20 each) on 1 April.

The following receipts and issues were recorded during April:

8 April	receives 600 units at $3.00 each
15 April	receives 400 units at $3.40 each
30 April	issues 925 units

4 What would be the value of the issues under LIFO?

    A $2,935

    B $4,040

    C $2,932

    D $2,850

5 What would be the total value of issues under AVCO?

    A $2,935

    B $4,040

    C $2,932

    D $2,850

6 What would the total value of issues under FIFO?

    A $2,935

    B $4,040

    C $2,932

    D $2,850

For suggested answers, see the 'Answers' section at the end of the book.

Chapter 6

LABOUR COSTS

This chapter focuses on the methods of remuneration used to determine gross pay in relation to both wages and salaries. The chapter covers syllabus areas B1(c), C1(c) and D2(a–d)

CONTENTS

1   Recording labour costs

2   Calculating gross pay – time related pay

3   Calculating gross pay – output related pay

4   Bonus schemes

5   Salaried employees – bonuses

6   Time rate employees – bonuses

7   Group bonus schemes

8   The impact of changes of remuneration methods on costs per unit

9   Payroll

10   Bookkeeping entries

11   Non-manufacturing organisations

12   Productivity

LEARNING OUTCOMES

On completion of this chapter the student should be able to:

- Describe the procedures and documentation to ensure the correct authorisation, coding, analysis and recording of direct and indirect labour and expenses.

- Describe and illustrate the classification of labour costs.

- Describe and illustrate the accounting for labour costs (including overtime premiums and idle time).

- Prepare an analysis of gross and net earnings.

- Explain and illustrate labour remuneration methods.

- Calculate the effect of remuneration methods and changes in productivity on unit labour costs.

1 RECORDING LABOUR COSTS

1.1 EMPLOYEE PERSONNEL RECORDS

When an employee joins an organisation it must record details of the employee, their job and pay. This is done by the Human Resources (personnel) department in the individual employee's personnel record.

Details that might be kept about an employee are as follows:

- full name, address and date of birth

- personal details such as marital status and emergency contact name and address

- benefit contribution number

- previous employment history

- educational details

- professional qualifications

- date of joining organisation

- employee number or code

- clock number issued

- job title and department

- rate of pay agreed

- holiday details agreed

- bank details if salary is to be paid directly into bank account

- amendments to any of the details above (such as increases in agreed rates of pay)

- date of termination of employment (when this takes place) and reasons for leaving.

1.2 EMPLOYEE RECORD OF ATTENDANCE

On any particular day an employee may be at work, on holiday, absent due to sickness or absent for some other reason. A record must be kept of these details for each day.

This information about an employee's attendance will come from various sources such as clock cards, time sheets, job sheets, and job cards.

1.3   HOLIDAY

Employees have an agreed number of days holiday per year. This will usually be paid holiday for salaried employees but may well be unpaid for employees paid by results or on time rates.

It is important for the employer to keep a record of the days of holiday taken by the employee to ensure that the agreed number of days per year are not exceeded.

1.4   SICKNESS

The organisation will have its own policies regarding payment for sick leave as well as legal requirements for statutory sick pay. Therefore, it is necessary to keep a record of the number of days of sick leave each year for each employee.

1.5   OTHER PERIODS OF ABSENCE

A record needs to be kept of any other periods of absence by an employee. These might be perfectly genuine such as jury service or training courses or alternatively unexplained periods of absence that must be investigated.

1.6   CLOCK CARDS

Definition   A **clock card** is a document which records the starting and finishing time for an employee (for example, 9 till 5.30).

There is usually some form of electronic or computerised recording system, so that when the employee's clock card is entered into the machine the time is recorded. This will give the starting and finishing time for the day and also in some systems the break times taken. Not all organisations will have these; they are mainly used in **factories** for shift work.

Clock cards are used as a source document in the calculation of the employee's gross pay.

1.7   TIME SHEETS

Definition   A **time sheet** is a record of how a person's time at work has been spent.

The total hours that an employee has worked in a day or week are shown on the employee's clock card but a breakdown of how those hours were spent is shown on the time sheet.

Each employee fills out a time sheet on a daily, weekly or monthly basis depending upon the policies of the organisation.

The employee enters their name, clock number and department at the top of the time sheet together with details of the work carried out in the period and the hours spent on that work.

This enables the cost of each employee's labour to be correctly charged to the appropriate production cost centre.

There will usually be a category for 'idle time' or administration time to recognise that not all time may be involved in production.

Definition **Idle time** is the hours for which an employee is available and being paid, but during which no output is being achieved, for example due to machine breakdown or a shortage of work or materials.

Excessive idle time payments reflect inefficiencies in the production operations and it is important therefore that idle time is separately recorded and monitored and kept to a minimum.

Idle time payments, whether paid to direct employees or to indirect employees, are normally classified as indirect labour costs.

1.8 JOB SHEETS

Definition A **job sheet** records the number of each type of product that an employee has produced in the period.

Time sheets are prepared by employees who are paid for the number of hours that they work. However it is also possible to pay employees on the basis of the number of units of a product they produce, known as a results or **piece rate basis**.

For an employee paid on the basis of the number of products produced a time sheet is of little use. Instead, such an employee would complete some form of job sheet, which is used to calculate their gross pay.

Payment to the employee will then be based upon the information on this job sheet.

Conclusion In order to correctly charge each cost centre for labour costs and calculate the correct amount of gross pay it is vital that the labour cost documentation is accurately completed.

2 CALCULATING GROSS PAY – TIME RELATED PAY

There are two main methods of calculating the gross pay of employees:

- pay employees for the time spent at work (time related pay)

- pay employees for the work actually produced (**output related pay**).

2.1 TIME RELATED PAY

Employees paid under a time related pay method are paid for the hours that they spend at work regardless of the amount of production or output that they achieve in that time. Time related pay employees can be split into two types, **salaried employees** and **hourly rate employees**.

2.2 SALARIED EMPLOYEES

Definition A **salaried employee** is one whose gross pay is agreed at a fixed amount for a period of time whatever hours that employee works in that period.

This might be expressed as an annual salary such as $18,000 per year or as a weekly rate such as $269.50 per week.

Each organisation will have a set number of hours that are expected to be worked each week, for example a standard working week of 37.5 hours, and salaried employees will be expected to work for at least this number of hours each week.

However if the salaried employee works for more than the standard number of hours for the week then the employment agreement may specify that overtime payments are to be made for the additional hours.

2.3 HOURLY RATE EMPLOYEES

Definition   An **hourly rate employee** is one who is paid a set hourly rate for each hour worked.

These employees are paid for the actual number of hours of attendance in a period, usually a week. A rate of pay will be set for each hour of attendance.

2.4 OVERTIME

Definition   **Overtime** is the number of hours worked by an employee which is greater than the number of hours set by the organisation as the working week.

It is common that employees that work overtime are paid an additional amount per hour for those extra hours.

2.5 OVERTIME PREMIUM

Definition   **Overtime premium** is the amount over and above the normal hourly rate that employees are paid for overtime hours.

ACTIVITY 1

An employee's basic week is 40 hours at a rate of pay of $10 per hour. Overtime is paid at a premium of 50% over the basic rate, also known as 'time and a half'.

The employee works a 45-hour week.

What is the total gross pay for this employee for the week?

Distinguish between the overtime payment and overtime premium for the week.

For a suggested answer, see the 'Answers' section at the end of the book.

Overtime premium paid to direct employees may be classified as a direct cost or as an indirect cost depending on the circumstances that cause the overtime to be worked.

- The premium paid for overtime that is worked because of a general increased level of activity in the organisation is classified as an indirect cost or overhead. This is because it would not be 'fair' to charge extra direct labour cost to a cost unit that just happens to be worked on during overtime hours.

- The premium paid for overtime that is worked at the specific request of a customer is charged as a direct labour cost to that customer's order. In this case the extra cost of the overtime hours can be traced to a specific cost unit. Therefore the overtime premium is classified as a direct cost of that order.

Example

The wages cost incurred last period included the following items:

	$
Direct wages paid – basic rate	23,000
Overtime premium paid to direct workers	2,900
Indirect wages paid – basic rate	14,000
Overtime premium paid to indirect workers	3,100

How much would be classified as indirect wages (overhead) for the period?

Solution

We will assume that the overtime was not worked at the specific request of a customer and therefore that all overtime premium should be treated as an indirect labour cost or overhead.

Indirect labour cost = $(2,900 + 14,000 + 3,100) = $20,000

3 CALCULATING GROSS PAY – OUTPUT RELATED PAY

Output related pay is also known as payment by results or piecework. This is a direct alternative to time related pay.

Definition **Payment by results or piecework** is where a fixed amount is paid per unit of output achieved irrespective of the time spent.

ACTIVITY 2

If the amount paid to an employee is $3 per unit produced and that employee produces 80 units in a week how much would his gross pay be?

For a suggested answer, see the 'Answers' section at the end of the book.

3.1 ADVANTAGES OF PAYMENT BY RESULTS

As far as an employee is concerned, payment by results means that they can earn whatever they wish within certain parameters. The harder they work and the more units they produce the higher the wage earned.

From the employer's point of view higher production or output can also be encouraged with a system of differential piecework.

3.2 PROBLEMS WITH PAYMENT BY RESULTS

There are **two** main problems associated with payment by results. One is the problem of accurate recording of the actual output produced. The amount claimed to be produced determines the amount of pay and, therefore, is potentially open to abuse unless it can be adequately supervised. A system of job sheets and checking of job sheets needs to be in place.

The second problem is that of the maintenance of the quality of the work. If the employee is paid by the amount that is produced then the temptation might be to produce more units but of a lower quality.

For these reasons basic piecework systems are rare in practice – variations of these systems are used instead.

3.3   PIECE RATE WITH GUARANTEE

A **piece rate with guarantee** gives the employee some security if the employer does not provide enough work in a particular period. The way that the system works is that if an employee's earnings for the amount of units produced in the period are lower than the guaranteed amount then the guaranteed amount is paid instead.

ACTIVITY 3

Jones is paid $6.00 for every unit that he produces but he has a guaranteed wage of $50.00 per eight-hour day. In a particular week he produces the following number of units:

Monday	12 units
Tuesday	14 units
Wednesday	8 units
Thursday	14 units
Friday	10 units

Calculate Jones's wage for this week.

For a suggested answer, see the 'Answers' section at the end of the book.

3.4   DIFFERENTIAL PIECEWORK

Definition   A **differential piecework** system is where the piece rate increases as successive targets for a period are achieved and exceeded.

This will tend to encourage higher levels of production and acts as a form of bonus payment for employees who produce more units than the standard level.

The system can work in one of two ways:

- the differential rate can be applied to all output produced, or

- the differential rate is applied to excess output over the previous threshold.

Most organisations' agreements would apply the second method.

Exam questions will state clearly which method should be used.

ACTIVITY 4

Payment by results rates for an organisation are as follows:

Up to 99 units per week	$1.25 per unit
100 to 119 units per week	$1.50 per unit
120 or more units per week	$1.75 per unit

If an employee produces 102 units in a week, how much will he be paid if the differential rate applies to:

(a)   the total output produced

(b)   the excess output over the previous threshold.

For a suggested answer, see the 'Answers' section at the end of the book.

4   BONUS SCHEMES

Bonuses may be paid to employees for a variety of reasons. An individual employee, a department, a division or the entire organisation may have performed particularly well and it is felt by the management that a bonus is due to some or all of the employees.

4.1   BASIC PRINCIPLE OF BONUSES

The basic principle of a bonus payment is that the employee is rewarded for any additional income or savings in cost to the organisation. This may be, for example, because the employee has managed to save a certain amount of time on the production of a product or a number of products. This time saving will save the organisation money and the amount saved will tend to be split between the organisation and the employee on some agreed basis. The amount paid to the employee/employees is known as the **bonus**.

4.2   METHOD OF PAYMENT

The typical bonus payable will often depend on the method of payment of the employee. The calculation and payment of bonuses will differ for salaried employees, employees paid by results and employees paid on a time rate basis.

5   SALARIED EMPLOYEES – BONUSES

Salaried employees are paid a predetermined salary or wage every week or every month. It may also be the organisation's policy to pay employees a bonus each month, quarter or annually.

5.1   CALCULATION OF BONUS

The calculation of the amount of bonus to be paid to each individual will depend upon the policy of the organisation. The policy may be to assign the same amount of bonus to each employee or alternatively to base the amount of each individual employee's bonus on the amount of their salary.

5.2 FLAT RATE BONUS

Definition A **flat rate bonus** is where all employees are paid the same amount of bonus each regardless of their individual salary.

The principle behind such a payment is that all of the employees have contributed the same amount to earning the bonus no matter what their position in the organisation or their salary level.

ACTIVITY 5

Suppose that a small business made a profit of $100,000 in the previous quarter and the managing director decided to pay out $20,000 of this as a flat rate bonus to each employee. The business has 50 employees in total including the managing director earning a salary of $48,000 per annum and Chris Roberts his secretary who earns $18,000 per annum.

How much would the managing director and Chris Roberts each receive as bonus for the quarter?

For a suggested answer, see the 'Answers' section at the end of the book.

5.3 PERCENTAGE BONUS

The alternative method of calculating the bonus due to each employee is to base it upon the annual salary of each employee.

Definition A **percentage bonus** is where the amount paid to each employee as bonus is a set percentage of that employee's annual salary.

The principle behind this method of calculating the bonus is to give a larger bonus to those with higher salaries in recognition that they have contributed more to the earning of the bonus than those with a lower salary.

ACTIVITY 6

Using the previous example again, a small business made a profit of $100,000 in the previous quarter and the managing director decided to pay out $20,000 of this as a bonus to employees. The business has 50 employees in total including the managing director earning a salary of $48,000 per annum and Chris Roberts his secretary who earns $18,000 per annum.

The bonus for each employee is to be calculated as 1.6% of each employee's annual salary.

How much would the managing director and Chris Roberts each receive as bonus for the quarter?

For a suggested answer, see the 'Answers' section at the end of the book.

6 TIME RATE EMPLOYEES – BONUSES

Employees paid on a time rate basis are paid a certain amount per hour regardless of the amount produced in that hour. Therefore, hardworking employees are paid the same as less hardworking employees.

The principle of a bonus or incentive scheme for time rate paid employees is to encourage them to achieve additional output in the time they work.

6.1 BASIS OF BONUS SCHEMES

The basis of bonus schemes in these instances is to set a predetermined standard time (or target time) for the performance of a job or production of a given amount of output. If the job is completed in less than the standard time or more than the given output is achieved in the standard time then this will mean additional profit to the employer.

Definition **Individual bonus schemes** are those that benefit individual workers according to their own results.

This additional profit earned by the individual employee will then be split between the employer and the employee in some agreed manner.

ACTIVITY 7

It is expected that it will take 90 minutes for an employee to make one unit of a product. If the employee makes one unit of the product in 60 minutes, what is the labour cost saving to the employer if the employee's wage rate is $10.00 per hour?

For a suggested answer, see the 'Answers' section at the end of the book.

6.2 PAYMENT TO EMPLOYEES UNDER A BONUS SCHEME

The manner in which the time saved is to be split between the employer and employee is stated in the employee's contract of employment. The precise terms could be a matter of negotiation between both parties. One approach would be to split the benefit of the time saving equally between the employee and employer.

The formula that is used to calculate this is:

$$\text{Bonus} = \frac{(\text{Time allowed} - \text{Time taken}) \times \text{Rate paid}}{2}$$

ACTIVITY 8

Employee's basic rate	$12 per hour
Allowed time for job A	1 hour and
Time taken for job A	36 minutes

What is the total amount that the employee will earn for job A if the bonus is calculated so as to share the benefit of the time saved equally?

For a suggested answer, see the 'Answers' section at the end of the book.

As an alternative, the proportion of the time saving paid to the employee could be based on the ratio of time taken to time allowed.

The formula to calculate this is:

$$\text{Bonus} = \frac{\text{Time taken}}{\text{Time allowed}} \times \text{Time saved} \times \text{Rate paid}$$

ACTIVITY 9

Employee's basic rate	$12 per hour
Allowed time for job A	1 hour
Time taken for job A	36 minutes

What is the total amount that the employee will earn for job A if the bonus is calculated based upon the ratio of time taken to time allowed?

For a suggested answer, see the 'Answers' section at the end of the book.

The structure of any bonus scheme is really a matter for management to decide. There may be a danger that providing too much encouragement to work faster will harm the company. For example, output might be rushed and mistakes might be made. An incentive scheme that encourages harmful behaviour is said to be 'dysfunctional'.

7 GROUP BONUS SCHEMES

Definition A **group bonus scheme** is where the bonus is based upon the output of the workforce as a whole or a particular group of the workforce. The bonus is then shared between the individual members of the group on some pre-agreed basis.

7.1 ADVANTAGES OF A GROUP SCHEME

A group scheme has a number of advantages over individual schemes:

- 'group loyalty' may result in less absenteeism and lateness

- it is not necessary to record the output of each individual worker, therefore it is an easier system to operate and control

- in a production line situation where the speed of the output is determined by the speed of the production line then a group scheme is more appropriate than an individual scheme.

ACTIVITY 10

Ten employees work as a group. The standard output for the group is 200 units per hour and when this is exceeded each employee in the group is paid a bonus in addition to the hourly wage.

The bonus percentage is calculated as follows:

$$50\% \times \frac{\text{Excess units}}{\text{Standard units}}$$

Each employee in the group is then paid as a bonus this percentage of an hourly wage rate of $10 no matter what the individual's hourly wage rate is.

The following is one week's record of production by the group:

	Hours worked	Production units
Monday	90	24,500
Tuesday	88	20,600
Wednesday	90	24,200
Thursday	84	20,100
Friday	88	20,400
Saturday	40	10,200
	480	120,000

(a)   What is the rate of the bonus per hour and what is the total bonus to be split between group members?

(b)   If Jones worked for 42 hours and was paid $8 per hour as a basic rate what would be his total pay for this week?

For a suggested answer, see the 'Answers' section at the end of the book.

8   THE IMPACT OF CHANGES OF REMUNERATION METHODS ON COSTS PER UNIT

8.1   REMUNERATION METHODS AND COST BEHAVIOUR

In chapter 3 we saw how various types of cost behaviour translated into different cost per unit behaviours.

The different remuneration methods discussed in this chapter can be correlated to these cost behaviours as follows:

Fixed costs

A good example of a purely fixed cost would be for employees paid a straight salary with no element, such as a bonus, that relates to output.

Fixed salary – cost per unit

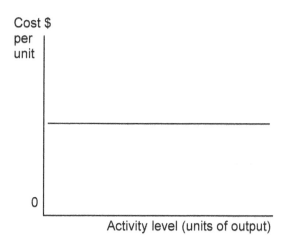

Variable costs

A good example of a variable cost would be for employees paid under a piece rate system with no guaranteed minimum payment

Piece rate scheme – cost per unit

A differential piece rate scheme would also be a variable cost but the cost per unit would not necessarily be a straight line as above.

Differential piece rate scheme – cost per unit

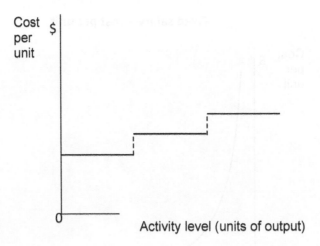

Semi-variable cost per unit

A good example of a semi-variable cost would be for employees paid under a piece rate system with a guaranteed minimum payment

Piece rate scheme with guarantee – cost per unit

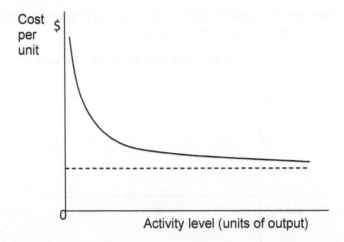

8.2 CHANGING REMUNERATION METHODS

If the remuneration method is changed then the cost per unit figure and behaviour may change.

For example, switching from a simple piece work system to one with a guarantee will change the cost behaviour from purely variable to semi-variable..

9 PAYROLL

9.1 INITIAL RECORDING OF GROSS PAY

The initial calculation and recording of gross pay for employees will be done in the payroll department. This department will then also calculate any income tax deductions under PAYE (Pay As You Earn) and the employees' benefit contribution contributions and any further deductions in order to determine the net pay for each employee for the period. Employers are responsible for collecting these taxes from employees and for remitting those deductions to the government. Other deductions may be mandatory, such as the employees' contribution to their pension fund, or voluntary, such as membership fees for trade unions.

The department will also calculate the employer's benefit contribution for each employee, which is an additional cost to be borne by the employer.

We can illustrate how gross pay becomes net pay in the following table:

	$
Employee's gross pay	X
Less: PAYE	(X)
Less: employee's benefit contributions	(X)
Net pay	**XX**

Example – gross pay and net pay

The payroll department has produced the following information for the month of May about the pay for employees in department M.

Department M	$
Payments to employees	15,000
Income tax	5,000
Employees' benefit contribution	3,400
Employer's benefit contribution	4,000

The gross wages are calculated as follows:

Department M	$
Payments to employees	15,000
Income tax	5,000
Employees' benefit contribution	3,400
Gross pay	**23,400**

The **net pay** is simply the payments to employees ($15,000).

The labour cost for department M for the month of May is calculated as follows:

Gross pay	23,400
Employer's benefit contribution	4,000
Labour cost – department M	**27,400**

Note that the income tax and employees' benefit contribution contributions have already been deducted from gross pay and so have already been accounted for.

9.2 CODING OF LABOUR COSTS

Payroll calculations are necessary in order to pay employees the correct amounts and to record the correct gross pay figure for financial accounting purposes.

However for cost accounting purposes more detail is needed. It is important that the gross pay of each employee is coded so that it is charged to the correct production cost centre.

In some instances an employee's clock card or time sheet might show that he worked for different cost centres during the period and therefore the gross pay must be broken down into the amount to be charged to each cost centre and correctly coded as such.

9.3 SERVICE COST CENTRE EMPLOYEES

The employees of a manufacturing organisation do not all work for cost centres that actually produce the products. Many employees will work in service cost centres such as stores, the canteen, the accounts department and the sales division.

Costs need to be recognised by each of these service cost centres and therefore the gross pay of these employees must also be coded to show which cost centre they have worked for in the period.

10 BOOKKEEPING ENTRIES

10.1 THE PROCESS OF ACCOUNTING FOR LABOUR COSTS

In a cost accounting system, **transactions involving labour costs** are recorded in a **wages and salaries control account**. This account records the total cost of wages and salaries, and is used to charge these costs to different departments, as either direct labour costs or indirect labour costs (overheads).

Example

A company has the following information

Transactions recorded in the period

Gross wages	$30,000
Of which direct wages are	$11,000
Indirect wages in production are	$7,000
Indirect wages in administration are	$4,000
Indirect wages in selling are	$8,000

This information can be used to prepare the cost accounts.

- Total wages costs for the period are debited to a wages and salaries control account

- The costs are then analysed according to whether they are direct or indirect costs. Direct costs are transferred to the WIP account and indirect costs are passed to the relevant overhead accounts. Normally you would not expect to see a closing balance on a wages account as all of the labour costs incurred are allocated in the period.

Wages and salaries control account

	$		$
Cost ledger control account	30,000	Work-in-progress	11,000
(*Total wages and salaries costs*)		(*Direct wages costs*)	
		Production overheads	7,000
		Admin overheads	4,000
		Selling/dist'n overheads	8,000
		(*Indirect labour costs*)	
	30,000		30,000

11 NON-MANUFACTURING ORGANISATIONS

Your syllabus does not concentrate solely on **manufacturing** organisations. It is also necessary to consider the costs that are incurred by **non-manufacturing** or service organisations.

11.1 SERVICE INDUSTRIES

Many organisations do not produce a physical cost unit or product. Instead, they provide a service.

This might be an accountant that provides a tax service for clients or a transport organisation which transports goods for customers.

In exactly the same way as manufacturing organisations these service industries need to gather together their costs for information and control purposes.

11.2 COSTS OF SERVICE INDUSTRIES

Many service industries will not have large costs relating to materials, for example an accountancy firm.

Many service costs will be **labour based**, with all of the problems of overtime, holiday pay, bonuses etc. involved in such costs.

Service industries will have many cost centres as in manufacturing organisations and relevant costs must be recognised for each cost centre.

11.3 COLLECTION, CLASSIFICATION AND ASCERTAINMENT OF COSTS

Costs will be classified under appropriate headings for the particular service. This will involve the issue of suitable cost codes for the recording and collection of costs. For example, for a transport company, the main cost classification may be based on the following activities:

- operating and running the fleet

- repairs and maintenance

- fixed charges

- administration.

Within each of these there would need to be a sub-classification of costs, each with its own code, so that under vehicle fixed costs, there might appear the following breakdown:

- road fund licences

- insurances

- depreciation

- vehicle testing fees

- others.

The cost centres that might be in existence for such an organisation might be:

- maintenance department

- operating departments – may be sub-divided into:

    - different types of operations such as long-haul and short-haul types

    - vehicle fixed costs department

    - canteen

    - administration, etc.

Conclusion   In service industries the labour cost is often the major cost of the organisation. The gross labour cost, with all of its elements, must be recognised by the cost centres that have used each employee in just the same way as in a manufacturing organisation.

12 PRODUCTIVITY

Definition   **Productivity** is the amount of output produced per labour hour.

If productivity increases the cost per unit of output will change in different ways depending on the remuneration methods.

12.1 TIME RELATED PAY AND PRODUCTIVITY

If the employee is paid on a time basis then by increasing productivity the labour cost per unit will fall.

Example

An employee is paid $6 per hour for a 38-hour week. In week 10 output per hour was 15 units. This increased to 17 units per hour in week 11. Show the impact on unit labour costs.

Solution

In week 10 unit labour cost is $6/15 = $0.40 per unit

In week 11 unit labour cost is $6/17 = $0.35 per unit

The labour cost per unit has fallen from $0.40 to $0.35. Managers may share some of this gain with employees in the form of a bonus.

12.2 OUTPUT RELATED PAY AND PRODUCTIVITY

If the employee is paid on an output basis, increasing productivity will have no effect on the unit labour cost for the organisation as a fixed rate is paid for each unit of output. In fact, the labour cost per unit may increase if a differential piecework system is used, as a higher fixed rate per unit may be paid for higher levels of production.

ACTIVITY 11

A differential piecework scheme specifies the following rates of pay per unit produced.

Up to 50 units per day $2 per unit

51 – 75 units per day $2.20 per unit

76 units or more per day $2.40 per unit

Only additional units qualify for the higher rate.

Calculate the labour cost per unit if production per day is:

(a)   45 units

(b)   80 units.

For a suggested answer, see the 'Answers' section at the end of the book.

CONCLUSION

It is important that payroll costs are calculated correctly from relevant source documentation and then analysed and coded to the correct cost unit or cost centre. Management accountants rely on this data being correct in order to measure productivity and plan resources.

KEY TERMS

Clock card – a document which records the starting and finishing time for an employee.

Time sheet – a record of how a person's time at work has been spent.

Job sheet – records the number of each type of product that an employee has produced in the period.

Idle time – hours for which an employee is available and being paid, but during which no output is being achieved, for example due to machine breakdown or a shortage of work or materials.

Salaried employee – one whose gross pay is agreed at a fixed amount for a period of time whatever hours the employee works in that period.

Hourly rate employee – one who is paid a set hourly rate for each hour worked.

Overtime – the number of hours worked by an employee which is greater than the number of hours set by the organisation as the working week.

Overtime premium – the amount over and above the normal hourly rate that employees are paid for overtime hours.

Differential piecework system – where the piece rate increases as successive targets for a period are achieved and exceeded.

Flat rate bonus – where all employees are paid the same amount of bonus each regardless of their individual salary.

Percentage bonus – where the amount paid to each employee as a bonus is a set percentage of that employee's annual salary.

Individual bonus scheme – a bonus scheme that benefits individual workers according to their own results.

Group bonus scheme – where the bonus is based upon the output of the workforce as a whole or a particular group of the workforce. The bonus is then shared between the individual members of the group on some pre-agreed basis.

Productivity – the amount of output produced per labour hour.

SELF TEST QUESTIONS

		Paragraph
1	What document would an employee use to record his time so that an accurate charge can be made to a cost centre or cost unit?	1.7
2	Are idle time payments to direct employees classified as direct wages or as indirect wages?	1.7
3	In what circumstances are overtime premiums paid to direct employees classified as direct wages?	2.5
4	Define the term 'piecework' and explain briefly how it differs from a group bonus scheme.	3, 4

EXAM-STYLE QUESTIONS

1   James and Jake are both hourly paid employees with conditions as follows:

   - James works a basic 40-hour week at an hourly rate of $6.20. Overtime is paid at a premium of 50% over the basic rate (time and half) for week days and at a premium of 100% (double time) for weekends.

   - Jake works a basic 35-hour week at an hourly rate of $7.40. Overtime is paid at a premium of 50% over the basic rate for the first 6 hours and 100% thereafter.

   During a week James and Jake both worked for 48 hours, three of which were at the weekend, in the case of each employee.

   What is the gross pay for each employee for that week?

	James	Jake
A	$331.70	$392.20
B	$331.70	$429.20
C	$381.30	$392.20
D	$381.30	$429.20

The following information is relevant to questions 2 and 3.

A direct labour employee works a standard 37-hour week with any additional overtime being paid at a premium of 50% over the basic rate. The basic wage rate is $8 per hour.

2   In any week, if 40 hours were worked, what would the overtime premium be?

   A $320

   B $36

   C $24

   D $12

3   In any week, if 40 hours were worked of which 6 hours were idle time, what would the total direct and indirect labour costs be?

	Direct	Indirect
A	$332	Nil
B	$296	$36
C	$272	$60
D	$248	$84

4   A differential piecework scheme specifies the following rates:

Up to 49 units per week	$2.25 per unit
50 to 79 units per week	$2.50 per unit
80 or more units per week	$2.75 per unit

Only additional units qualify for the higher rate.

If an employee produces 86 units in a week, how much will he be paid?

A $185.75

B $204.00

C $204.50

D $236.50

5   An employee's basic rate is $6.80 per hour with a typical working week of 35 hours.

The time allowed for Product X is 48 minutes per unit.

In week 23 the employee managed to make 54 product Xs in 37 hours. The employer and the employee divide the benefit of the time saved equally between them.

What is the total amount that the employee will earn for the week?

A $259.08

B $270.64

C $272.68

D $293.76

6   The following information was recorded on the June payroll:

Salaries paid to employees	$2,500
Employees' NI contributions	$250
Income tax	$375
Employer's NI contributions	$280

What is the employees' gross pay for June?

A $2,500

B $2,750

C $3,125

D $3,405

For suggested answers, see the 'Answers' section at the end of the book.

Chapter 7

EXPENSES AND ABSORPTION OF OVERHEADS

This chapter explains and gives examples of expenses and their accounting treatment. Depreciation is an important expense which can be calculated in different ways. The concept of absorbing costs is also covered. This chapter covers syllabus areas B1(c), C1(e), D3(a and b).

CONTENTS

LEARNING OUTCOMES

On completion of this chapter the student should be able to:

*   Describe the procedures and documentation to ensure the correct authorisation, coding, analysis and recording of expenses.

*   Explain the process of charging indirect costs to cost centres and units including cost apportionment for indirect costs (excluding reciprocal service).

*   Explain and illustrate the process of cost absorption for indirect costs including the analysis and interpretation of over/under absorption.

*   Calculate the cost of a product or service.

1 CODING, ANALYSIS AND RECORDING OF EXPENSES

In cost accounting terms there are three types of business expenditure: materials, labour and expenses.

Definition **Expenses** are all business costs that are not classified as materials or labour costs.

It is possible to identify direct expenses, for example the cost of a royalty paid for each unit of output produced or the cost of a machine hired to complete a particular job. These expenses are direct because they can be identified with specific cost units.

However, the majority of expense items cannot be traced to a specific cost unit and they are therefore classified as indirect expenses or overheads.

1.1 TYPES OF EXPENSE

An organisation will incur many different types of indirect expense or overhead. There may be expenses associated with the manufacturing process or the factory, the selling process, general administration or day-to-day running and financing of the business.

Manufacturing expenses – examples

Examples of expenses incurred during the manufacturing process are:

- sub-contractors' costs

- the power for the machinery

- the lighting and heating of the factory

- insurance of the machinery

- cleaning of the factory and machines

- depreciation of the machinery.

Selling expenses – examples

When selling goods to customers the expenses that might be incurred are:

- advertising costs

- depreciation of packing machine

- costs of delivering the goods to the customer

- commission paid to sales representatives

- costs of after sales care

- warehouse rental for storage of goods.

Administration expenses – examples

The everyday running of the organisation will involve many different expenses including the following:

- rent of buildings

- business rates on buildings

- insurance of the buildings

- telephone bills

- postage and fax costs

- computer costs

- stationery

- costs of providing a canteen for the employees

- auditor's fees.

Finance expenses – examples

The costs of financing an organisation might include the following:

- loan interest

- lease charges if any equipment or buildings are leased rather than purchased.

1.2 CAPITAL EXPENDITURE AND REVENUE EXPENDITURE

Another important classification of expenses is the distinction between capital expenditure and revenue expenditure.

Capital expenditure is the expenditure arising when non-current (fixed) assets are purchased by an organisation. Capital expenditure is not charged to the income statement as an expense but is instead written off as a **depreciation charge** over the useful life of the asset. The depreciation charge is therefore charged to the income statement at the end of an accounting period.

Revenue expenditure is the expenditure incurred on 'everyday' items such as the running costs of fixed assets and other general expenses such as rent, rates, insurance and so on. Revenue expenditure is written off to the income statement in the period to which it relates.

Example – capital expenditure and revenue expenditure

An organisation purchased a building for $240,000 ten years ago. Five years later it added an extension to the original building at a cost of $75,000. General wear and tear of the building has resulted in maintenance costs of $2,750 being incurred in the current year.

Identify which of the costs incurred by the organisation are capital expenditure and which are revenue expenditure.

Solution

Capital expenditure amounts to $315,000 ($240,000 + $75,000). The maintenance costs of $2,750 are revenue expenditure and are written off in the income statement in the period to which they relate.

Conclusion

Capital expenditure and revenue expenditure are distinguished by the way in which they are accounted for in the income statement and the balance sheet (statement of financial position). Capital items are written off in the income statement via a depreciation charge and revenue items are written off in full in the period to which they relate.

2 COST CENTRES AND EXPENSES

It is important to bear in mind that the manner in which costs are recorded and associated with individual cost centres and units of production is largely a matter for management to decide in terms of what is best for the business. The manner in which cost centres are defined could have implications for the information that is generated by the costing records. For example, a business might treat its factory as a cost centre. That would mean that all manufacturing costs were added together. It would, however, be perfectly possible to divide the factory up into two or more cost centres. For example, if there are three production lines then the factory could treat each one as a separate manufacturing cost centre. Activities common to all three production lines, such as maintenance or health and safety, could then be treated as service cost centres within the manufacturing process.

In general, it will be cheaper and easier to run a system where there are fewer cost centres. However, there may be a drawback to that because management may not be able to identify the overall effect of certain activities on the business as a whole. For example, it may be that one of the company's products costs more to make than was first estimated. The organisation may decide to raise selling prices or to withdraw the product altogether. Unfortunately, it is rarely possible to predict the value of any additional information that might be obtained from changing or improving the system.

The subdivision of larger cost centres is not restricted to the manufacturing function. The sales function might be treated as a single cost centre or it may be broken down into different regions (e.g. home sales and export sales) or into different products (e.g. consumer products and industrial products). Similarly, administration could be subdivided into the accounts department, personnel, head office and so on.

2.1 TYPES OF EXPENSES

The various expenses of a business can be split into two types for basic costing purposes: expenses that can be directly attributed to a **single cost centre** and expenses that need to be shared between a **number of cost centres**. Whether an individual expense needs to be shared out or not depends on how the cost centres are organised. If there is more than one manufacturing cost centre then the cost of cleaning the factory will have to be shared out between them. If the factory is a single cost centre then it will not be shared out.

2.2 DIRECTLY ATTRIBUTABLE EXPENSES

The process of allotting a whole item of overhead cost to a cost centre is called **allocation**. For example, if the whole of the sales function is a single cost centre then sales commission paid to sales staff will be directly attributable to that cost centre.

2.3 APPORTIONMENT OF EXPENSES

If you look at the list of administration expenses (given above) you will realise that many of these relate to a number of different cost centres. For example, the rent of the buildings will relate to the manufacturing cost centre(s), the sales department cost centre(s), the accounting cost centre and the canteen cost centre. This also applies to other expenses such as rates, insurance, electricity bills and telephone bills.

These joint expenses must therefore be shared out between each of the cost centres that incur some of these expenses in a fair manner. This process is known as **apportionment**.

2.4 EXPENSE APPORTIONMENT BASES

In order to apportion these expenses to cost centres fairly, a suitable basis of apportionment must be applied. Most organisations set out bases of apportionment in their policy manuals and these must be applied consistently. The apportionment bases used should be logical so that cost centre managers do not feel as though they are being treated unfairly. However, this should be balanced against the need to avoid making things unduly complex.

For example the **rent, rates and insurance** of the buildings may be apportioned to cost centres on the basis of the amount of **floor area** that each cost centre occupies. Similarly, **computer costs** might be apportioned on the basis of the **number of computer hours** that are used by each cost centre. The selection of these bases is not an exact science!

Example

Suppose that the rent, rates and buildings insurance for an organisation total $100,000. The floor space occupied by the five cost centres in the organisation is as follows:

	Square metres
Manufacturing cost centre	5,000
Stores cost centre	2,000
Canteen cost centre	1,500
Sales department cost centre	500
Administration cost centre	1,000
	10,000

Apportion the rent, rates and insurance overheads to each cost centre on the basis of floor space occupied.

Solution

		$
Manufacturing	($100,000 × 5,000/10,000)	50,000
Stores	($100,000 × 2,000/10,000)	20,000
Canteen	($100,000 × 1,500/10,000)	15,000
Sales	($100,000 × 500/10,000)	5,000
Administration	($100,000 ×1,000/10,000)	10,000
		100,000

2.5 CODING

In order to ensure that the correct amount of overhead is charged to each cost centre, apportionments need to be coded carefully so that the amount to be charged to each cost centre is clearly shown.

3 THE SELLING FUNCTION

Most organisations will have some form of **sales department** which will take orders for the sales of the goods that have been manufactured or the services that the business provides.

3.1 DUTIES OF THE SALES FUNCTION

The sales function of an organisation will typically be responsible for the following:

* processing orders from customers

* negotiating the details of the order

* notifying the production department of the order details

* preparing the despatch note for the goods

* preparing the sales invoices

* coding sales invoices

* organising any necessary advertising.

3.2 MAKE UP OF THE SALES FUNCTION

In many organisations the sales may be made largely by telephone. A customer will telephone with an order and this will then be processed by sales department personnel and an order confirmation sent out to the customer.

In other cases the sales function may be made up largely of travelling sales representatives who take orders personally from customers and then pass on the details to the sales department at head office for processing.

3.3 THE SALES FUNCTION AS A COST CENTRE

Just as with any other area of the business that incurs costs, for cost accounting purposes the sales department may well be classified as a cost centre.

Costs of selling

The typical costs that might be incurred in the sales cost centre are labour costs and expenses.

Labour costs

The labour costs incurred will be the gross pay of all of the people who work in the sales department. This may be telephone sales personnel or travelling sales representatives. The payroll should code the gross pay of each employee in the sales cost centre to the sales cost centre.

The gross pay of sales personnel may also include a particular type of bonus known as a sales commission. This may be based upon a fixed amount per order generated by a sales person or it may be based upon a percentage of the value of each order.

Expenses – selling and distribution overhead

The sales department will also incur a variety of expenses that must be charged to the sales cost centre. These might include the following:

- **advertising costs** – these should be coded as selling costs when the invoice is received

- **transport expenses of delivering the goods to customers** – these will include petrol, insurance of the vehicles and also depreciation of the delivery vehicles

- **telephone costs** – a proportion of the organisation's telephone bill will be apportioned to the sales cost centre

- **travelling expenses for the sales representatives** – these might include petrol, insurance and depreciation for the fleet of cars as well as any other incidental expenses such as overnight accommodation – all invoices and expense claims should be coded as costs for the sales cost centre.

3.4 THE SALES FUNCTION AS A PROFIT CENTRE

In some organisations the sales function may be treated as a profit centre rather a cost centre. This would mean that the income of the sales department would be the sales that are made and the costs would be the labour and expenses and probably also a cost for the value of the goods that are being sold.

Value of goods

If the sales function is to be treated as a profit centre then it is likely that it will effectively be charged with the cost of the goods that it is selling. This cost will be the total manufacturing cost of the goods, as determined by the management accountant, plus possibly a small profit element, or the purchase price, if finished goods are bought in.

Sales income

The income of the sales function will be derived from the sales value of the sales that it makes. This figure will be allocated to the sales profit centre by coding sales invoices not only to show the goods that have been sold and to which customer but also to indicate that the value of the invoice should be credited to the sales profit centre for costing purposes. This will allow analysis of sales by product, by customer and by amount.

The sales figure that should be taken from the invoice is **after** any trade discounts but **before** adding any Sales Tax. Remember that Sales Tax is not part of sales income, it is simply a tax collected by the organisation on behalf of the government. (For example, in the United Kingdom, Sales Tax is collected by organisations and then passed on to Revenue & Customs.)

Example

The sales function of an organisation has incurred the following costs taken from invoices and expense claims for the month of May:

	$
Advertising	2,400
Delivery costs	12,800
Sales representatives' expenses	1,400

There is also a journal entry for depreciation of delivery vehicles for the month of $800 and depreciation of the sales representatives' cars of $350.

The gross pay of all the employees of the sales department for the month has been provided by the payroll department as $18,600 including sales commissions of $1,600.

The gross value of the sales including Sales Tax at 17½% made by the department for the month is $176,250.

The management accountant has valued the goods that were sold at a total manufacturing cost of $50,000.

What profit has been made by the sales function for the month?

Solution

	$	$
Sales (net of Sales Tax $176,250 × 100/117.5)		150,000
Costs:		
Cost of goods sold	50,000	
Labour cost	18,600	
Advertising	2,400	
Delivery costs	12,800	
Sales representatives' expenses	1,400	
Depreciation (800 + 350)	1,150	
		86,350
Profit		63,650

Conclusion

The sales function of an organisation incurs costs like any other department of the organisation. However it also earns income in the form of the sales that are made. Therefore it may be treated as a cost centre or alternatively as a profit centre.

4 ABSORPTION OF INDIRECT OR OVERHEAD COSTS

4.1 ALLOCATION AND APPORTIONMENT TO COST CENTRES

Direct labour, materials and expenses can be specifically allocated to cost units while indirect labour, materials and expenses must be allocated to overhead cost centres or apportioned between a number of different cost centres on an appropriate basis.

The process of allocation and apportionment requires that all production overheads are eventually assigned to a production cost centre.

A **production cost centre** is one that is directly involved with the production activity. Examples include the machining and assembly cost centres. A **service cost centre** is a centre whose activity supports that of the production cost centres but which does not produce any production output. Examples include maintenance, stores and administration.

After the initial process of allocation and apportionment of overheads, the total of the service cost centre overheads must be reapportioned to the production cost centres. This process of re-apportionment is necessary so that the total of the overhead costs can be absorbed into the cost of the output that passes through the production cost centres.

Example – allocation and apportionment

Overheads are analysed (i.e. allocated, apportioned and reapportioned) on an overhead analysis sheet.

OVERHEAD ANALYSIS SHEET		PERIOD ENDING				
	Total	Production cost centre X	Production cost centre Y	Production cost centre Z	Service cost centre 1	Service cost centre 2
	$	$	$	$	$	$
Allocated costs	100,000	34,000	32,000	21,000	10,000	3,000
Factory rent	12,400	3,100	5,200	2,700	1,200	200
Heating and lighting	2,500	700	1,200	200	300	100
Building repairs	5,600	1,300	1,700	2,600		
Insurance	8,000	2,100	4,800	1,100		
	128,500	41,200	44,900	27,600	11,500	3,300

The first line of the overhead analysis sheet shows the overheads that are allocated to the production and service cost centres. The other overheads (factory rent, heating and lighting, building repairs and insurance) are apportioned (i.e. shared out) between both production and service cost centres where relevant. The total overheads allocated and apportioned to the service cost centres ($11,500 to the service cost centre 1 and $3,300 to service cost centre 2) must be reapportioned between the production cost centres only.

Suppose service cost centre 1 works equally for production cost centres X and Y only. This will mean that $5,750 will be reapportioned to each of these production cost centres. Similarly, suppose that service cost centre 2 works equally for all three production cost centres, then $1,100 ($3,300/3) will be reapportioned to each production cost centre.

We can extend the overhead analysis sheet shown above to show the reapportionment of service cost centre overheads.

OVERHEAD ANALYSIS SHEET continued					PERIOD ENDING	
	Total	Production cost centre X	Production cost centre Y	Production cost centre Z	Service cost centre 1	Service cost centre 2
	$	$	$	$	$	$
Allocated and apportioned costs	128,500	41,200	44,900	27,600	11,500	3,300
Reapportionment of service cost centre 1		5,750	5,750		(11,500)	
Reapportionment of service cost centre 2		1,100	1,100	1,100		(3,300)
Total overhead		48,050	51,750	28,700		

4.2 TREATMENT OF OVERHEAD COSTS

The overheads incurred or apportioned to a production cost centre are the overheads incurred in producing the products that are made in that production cost centre. The overheads are a valid part of the product cost just like direct materials, direct labour and direct expenses. Therefore production cost centres' overhead costs must be absorbed by each individual product or cost unit in some way. This process is called **absorption**.

4.3 ABSORPTION OF OVERHEAD COSTS

Definition **Absorption of overhead costs** is a method of including a fair proportion of the total overhead costs in the cost of each cost unit.

Overheads are absorbed into cost units by sharing out overhead costs of a production cost centre for the period amongst the products (or cost units) actually produced in the period.

There are many different possible methods of achieving this absorption of costs.

4.4 ABSORPTION ON THE BASIS OF UNITS PRODUCED

The simplest method of estimating the amount of overhead to be included in the cost of each unit of production is to take the total estimated production overhead and divide it by the number of units expected to be produced in the period.

ACTIVITY 1

The total production overhead for the next month for a cost centre is estimated to be $40,000. In that month it is estimated that 80,000 products will be produced. What is the overhead absorption rate based upon the expected number of units to be produced?

For a suggested answer, see the 'Answers' section at the end of the book.

This is a simple and acceptable method of absorbing overheads as long as the cost units are identical, or similar. But if a range of products is made it is not fair if small or relatively inexpensive products absorb the same share of overheads as larger or more expensive products.

Conclusion   If an organisation produces just one product then it is acceptable to absorb overheads on the basis of units produced.

5   ABSORPTION OF OVERHEADS ON A TIME BASIS

5.1   NATURE OF OVERHEADS

Most overheads however are not dependent upon the number of units produced. In fact most overheads are probably more dependent upon the amount of time that elapses or the amount of time that is worked in a particular cost centre. For example rent paid is based on the amount of time that the premises are occupied, heating and lighting bills depend on the amount of time that the facilities are used and power for machinery depends on the amount of time that the machines are used.

Therefore some measure of time is often a better method of absorbing overheads into product costs rather than simply the number of units produced.

5.2   PROBLEM WITH THE NUMBER OF UNITS METHOD

The problem with the units of production approach to overhead absorption can be illustrated using the following example.

Suppose that the total production overheads of an organisation are again $40,000 and that the number of products produced is 80,000. These 80,000 products are made up of 40,000 units of product A and 40,000 units of product B.

Absorbing the production overheads on the basis of the number of units produced would lead to $0.50 per unit of overhead being included in the cost of units of both A and B.

Suppose however that product A requires 1 hour in the production cost centres whereas product B requires 20 hours.

In such a situation it would appear to be fair that product B absorbs more of the production overhead per unit than product A. Product B spends 20 times longer in production than product A and there ought to be some reflection of this in the sharing out of the production overheads between the products.

5.3 TIME BASIS FOR OVERHEAD ABSORPTION

If overheads are thought to be incurred on a time basis rather than a per unit basis then it is more appropriate to absorb overheads on the basis of the amount of time that they spend in each production cost centre. The two main measures of time in a production cost centre are labour hours and machine hours.

5.4 LABOUR HOURS BASIS FOR OVERHEAD ABSORPTION

One measure of the amount of time that a product spends in a production department (cost centre) is the standard labour hours due to be spent on that product in that department. In a labour intensive production environment the standard labour hours for a product might be the most appropriate method of absorbing the production overheads.

ACTIVITY 2

An organisation has a single production department which incurs expected overheads of $20,000 per annum. The estimated number of labour hours worked in the department are 80,000.

What is the overhead absorption rate per labour hour?

If a single unit of product J spends two hours in the production department, what is the amount of overhead to be included in the cost of one unit of product J?

For a suggested answer, see the 'Answers' section at the end of the book.

5.5 MACHINE HOURS

An alternative measure of the time spent in a department by a product is the number of machine hours spent.

In a machine-based or automated production environment the amount of machine time spent on a product is the best basis for absorbing the production overheads into each unit of production.

6 METHODS OF OVERHEAD ABSORPTION

6.1 INTRODUCTION

In the earlier part of this chapter the basic calculations of overhead absorption and a variety of different methods of determining absorption rates have been considered.

How an absorption costing system may work in practice to result in a full product cost per unit must now be considered.

6.2   BLANKET OVERHEAD ABSORPTION

Definition   In **blanket overhead absorption** the total production overheads of the organisation are absorbed on a single absorption basis.

This is by far the simplest method of overhead absorption as it does not require any allocation or apportionment of overheads to cost centres.

However this method does not take account of the different activities in each cost centre, nor of the different patterns of overhead costs incurred in each cost centre. Neither does it allow for the varying load that may be placed by each product on the facilities of each cost centre.

6.3   SEPARATE COST CENTRE OVERHEAD ABSORPTION RATES

Definition   **Cost centre overhead absorption** is where the total production overhead for each cost centre is determined separately using allocation and apportionment of overheads. Each cost centre's overhead is then absorbed into the products worked on in that cost centre using the most appropriate basis.

The main advantage of this approach is that the production overhead for each cost centre can be absorbed using the most appropriate basis for that cost centre. For example a labour intensive cost centre might use labour hours as the basis of absorption and an automated cost centre might use machine hours as the basis of absorption.

The main disadvantage of the method is the volume of calculations required to allocate, apportion and then finally absorb the overheads.

6.4   ACTUAL AND PREDETERMINED OVERHEAD ABSORPTION RATES

The purpose of absorbing production overheads into the cost of each cost unit of an organisation is to ensure that the full production cost of that product is known. If actual production overheads and actual levels of activity for a period were used to determine absorption rates then these calculations could not take place until after the end of the period when the actual costs and production details were known.

However it would be more useful to know the amount of overhead likely to be included in the cost of each product at the start of the period rather than at the end.

For that reason predetermined or budgeted figures are normally used to calculate absorption rates.

6.5   BUDGETING PROCESS

Before the start of each accounting period the budgets for that period are set. This will include the budgeted amount of production overhead for the period and the budgeted level of activity for the period. The level of activity may be measured in terms of number of units to be produced, number of labour or machine hours to be worked, and so on.

The budgeted figures for each of the expense items such as rent and rates, electricity, insurance and depreciation are allocated or apportioned to each cost centre. The budgeted service cost centre costs are then re-apportioned to production cost centres to give the estimated or budgeted overhead cost for each production cost centre.

6.6 PREDETERMINED OVERHEAD ABSORPTION RATE

The budgeted production overhead for each cost centre is then divided by the budgeted level of activity for each cost centre (i.e. budgeted number of units to be produced or labour hours to be worked or machine hours to be incurred) to give the budgeted or predetermined overhead absorption rate.

Managers then have a unit rate available for planning and for control purposes, and if necessary for pricing products and services during the period.

Conclusion The apportionment of overheads is normally done as part of the budgeting process and as such is based upon budgeted costs for each type of overhead expense. The setting of the overhead absorption rate is also normally done as part of the budgeting process and is based upon the budgeted production overhead and the budgeted level of activity. If a blanket rate of overhead absorption is to be used then this level of activity could be an overall budgeted number of units of production for the organisation. If separate cost centre overhead absorption rates are to be calculated then separate measures of budgeted production activity for the period, e.g. labour hours or machine hours, will be used for each cost centre.

6.7 UNDER- AND OVER-ABSORPTION OF PRODUCTION OVERHEAD

It is very unlikely that the forecasts for production overhead and activity levels used to determine the absorption rate will be 100% accurate. There will almost certainly be a different amount of overhead actually incurred and a different level of activity achieved. This leads to a situation of under- or over-absorption of overheads, where the amount of overhead absorbed into production is lower or higher than the overhead actually incurred.

Example – under/over-absorbed production overhead

The following data are available for Department A for the latest period:

	Budget	Actual
Production overhead	$80,000	$85,000
Machine hours	20,000	21,000

Production overheads are absorbed using a machine hour rate.

Calculate the amount of under- or over-absorbed overhead for the period.

Solution

Production overhead absorption rate	=	$80,000/20,000 machine hours
	=	$4 per machine hour
Production overhead absorbed during period	=	$4 × 21,000 actual hours
	=	$84,000
Production overhead incurred		$85,000
		———
Under-absorbed overhead		$1,000
		———

This under-absorbed overhead is transferred as a debit to the income statement at the end of the accounting period. If there had been over-absorbed overhead then the transfer would be a credit to the income statement at the end of the period. Similarly, if there had been under-absorbed overhead, then the transfer would be a debit (expense) to the income statement.

6.8 NON-PRODUCTION OVERHEADS

Overheads normally absorbed into the cost of products are production overheads. These are the overheads that have been dealt with so far in this chapter. However, there also other types of overhead, in particular:

- selling and distribution overheads

- administration overheads

- finance overheads.

It is also possible to include some or all of these overheads as part of the cost of the product or cost unit if the organisation wishes to determine the full cost of each cost unit.

If these non-production overheads are to be included in the cost of the cost units then they must be absorbed into the cost in a similar manner to the production overheads by using some suitable absorption basis such as a per unit basis or perhaps as a percentage of the production cost of the product.

Conclusion   It is also possible to absorb non-production overheads into the cost of cost units. However this is not a particularly common practice. The usual treatment for non-production overheads is to write them off as an expense or period cost in the income statement for the period.

ACTIVITY 3

Job no. 958 incurs the following costs during its completion in department X.

Direct materials	$270
Direct labour (14 hours)	$126
Hire of special machine	$150

Production overheads in department X are absorbed at a rate of $3 per direct labour hour.

General overheads are added to each job at a rate of 10% of total production cost.

Calculate the following costs for job no. 958:

(a)   prime cost or total direct cost

(b)   total production cost

(c)   total cost.

For a suggested answer, see the 'Answers' section at the end of the book.

7   BOOKKEEPING ENTRIES

In previous chapters we have seen how different elements of the cost bookkeeping system can be completed for materials and labour. Here we include other expenses and overheads and show how it all fits together.

7.1   THE PROCESS OF ACCOUNTING FOR INPUT COSTS

Materials costs, labour costs and other expenses

There are three basic components of cost:

- materials costs

- labour costs

- other expenses.

In a cost accounting system, **transactions involving materials costs** are recorded in a **stores control account**. These transactions are mainly the purchase of stores items and the issue of materials to various departments within the organisation. The stores account also records the value of opening inventory and closing inventory of materials at the beginning and end of each period. Inventory may be raw materials in a manufacturing environment or material inputs in a service environment.

Transactions involving labour costs are recorded in a **wages and salaries control account**. This account records the total cost of wages and salaries, and is used to charge these costs to different departments, as either direct labour costs or indirect labour costs (overheads).

If we assume for simplicity that all other expenses are treated as indirect costs or overheads, **transactions involving other expenses** are recorded in an overhead costs account.

Building up costs of final outputs

There are also accounts within a cost ledger for building up the costs of production and the cost of sales of the products manufactured or jobs carried out for customers. The accounts that are used to do this are:

- The **work-in-progress account**, which records the costs of items manufactured. The account records costs in total, but the costs might be broken down into the costs of individual jobs or processes or the costs of individual products. The opening balance and closing balance on this account at the start and end of a period represent the total cost of unfinished production. The cost of WIP will include raw materials, labour and overheads.

- The **finished goods account**, which records the cost of finished production that has not yet been sold to a customer

- The **cost of sales account**, which records the cost of finished production that has been sold to customers.

Similar accounts may be used to collect the cost of providing a service but there will be no finished goods account as it is not possible to hold inventory of finished services.

7.2   THE MAIN ACCOUNTS IN THE COST LEDGER

To understand a cost accounting system, you need to be familiar with the principles of double entry bookkeeping. The following example illustrates how the double entry in a cost ledger would be carried out.

Example

A company has the following information

Opening balances of:	Raw materials	$2,000
	Work-in-progress	$1,500
	Finished goods	$8,000

Transactions recorded in the period	
Material purchases	$40,000
Direct materials issued to production	$21,000
Indirect materials issued to production	$3,000
Indirect materials issued to administration	$6,000
Indirect materials issued to selling	$5,000
Gross wages	$30,000
Of which direct wages are	$11,000
Indirect wages in production are	$7,000
Indirect wages in administration are	$4,000
Indirect wages in selling are	$8,000
Indirect production expenses	$7,500
Indirect administration expenses	$10,000
Indirect selling expenses	$3,000
Overheads charged to production	$17,500
Production completed	$49,000
Production cost of goods sold	$52,000

This information can be used to prepare the cost accounts.

The main accounts in the cost ledger are illustrated below. There are different types of account.

- Asset accounts such as the stores control account, work-in-progress (WIP) account and finished goods account. These record the transactions relating to raw materials, partly finished goods and completed goods in a period. Often there is inventory of raw materials, partly finished goods and finished goods at the end of a period which result in a closing balance and a corresponding opening balance for the beginning of the next period. In our example you can see the opening balances recorded on the debit side of the accounts. Once all of the other transactions for the period have been recorded in these accounts, the closing balance can be calculated as a balancing figure on the credit side.

- Expense accounts such as wages and overheads accounts. The stores account also records any purchases of raw materials in the period. Total costs for the period are debited to these accounts. The costs are then analysed according to whether they are direct or indirect costs. Direct costs are transferred to the WIP account and indirect costs are passed to the relevant overhead accounts. Normally you would not expect to see a closing balance on a wages account as all of the labour costs incurred are allocated in the period. In our example you can see the costs incurred in the period debited to the stores, wages and overhead accounts. The analysis into direct and indirect costs and the resulting accounting treatment will be covered in more detail in later chapters.

In the example you can see that the WIP account collects all of the costs relating to the production of the cost units in the period. As the goods are completed the value of the finished goods is credited to the WIP account and debited to the finished goods account.

The cost of goods sold is then credited to the finished goods account and debited to the cost of sales account.

Stores control account

	$		$
Opening inventory	2,000	Work-in-progress	21,000
Cost ledger control account	40,000	*(Direct materials issued to*	
(Material purchases)		*production)*	
		Production overheads	3,000
		Admin overheads	6,000
		Selling/dist'n overheads	5,000
		(Indirect materials consumed)	
		Closing inventory (*Balancing figure*)	7,000
	42,000		42,000

Wages and salaries control account

	$		$
Cost ledger control account	30,000	Work-in-progress	11,000
(Total wages and salaries costs)		*(Direct wages costs)*	
		Production overheads	7,000
		Admin overheads	4,000
		Selling/dist'n overheads	8,000
		(Indirect labour costs)	
	30,000		30,000

Production overheads account

	$		$
OVERHEADS INCURRED		OVERHEADS ABSORBED TO PRODUCTION*	
Stores control account	3,000	Work-in-progress	17,500
(Indirect production materials costs)			
Wages and salaries control	7,000		
(Indirect production labour costs)			
Cost ledger control account	7,500		
(Other indirect expenses)			
	17,500		17,500

Administration overheads account

	$		$
Stores control account	6,000	Income statement	20,000
(*Indirect materials costs*)			
Wages and salaries control	4,000		
(*Admin labour costs*)			
Cost ledger control account	10,000		
(*Other indirect expenses*)			
	────		────
	20,000		20,000
	────		────

Selling and distribution overheads account

	$		$
Stores control account	5,000	Income statement	16,000
(*Indirect materials costs*)			
Wages and salaries control	8,000		
(*Sales and distribution labour costs*)			
Cost ledger control account	3,000		
(*Other indirect expenses*)			
	────		────
	16,000		16,000
	────		────

Work-in-progress (WIP) account

	$		$
Opening inventory	1,500	Finished goods	49,000
(*Unfinished production*)			
Stores control account	21,000		
(*Direct materials costs*)			
Wages and salaries control	11,000		
(*Direct labour costs*)			
Production overhead account	17,500	Closing inventory	2,000
(*Indirect production costs*)		(*Unfinished production – Balancing figure*)	
	────		────
	51,000		51,000
	────		────

Finished goods account

	$		$
Opening inventory *(Unsold finished production)*	8,000	Cost of sales *(Production cost of finished goods sold in the period)*	52,000
Work-in-progress *(Production completed in the period)*	49,000	Closing inventory *(Unsold finished production – balancing figure)*	5,000
	57,000		57,000

Cost of sales account

	$		$
Finished goods *(Production cost of finished goods sold in the period)*	52,000	Income statement	52,000
	52,000		52,000

CONCLUSION

Depreciation is an important indirect expense in an organisation which will be allocated and apportioned, as will all indirect costs, to cost centres. Cost centre overhead costs will then be absorbed using a pre-determined absorption rate.

KEY TERMS

Allocation – expenses are directly attributed to a single cost centre.

Apportionment – any joint expenses are split up in some equitable manner between each of the cost centres that incur some of these expenses.

Production cost centre – a cost centre that is directly involved with the production activity.

Service cost centre – a cost centre whose activity supports that of the production cost centres but which does not produce any production output.

Absorption – a method of including a fair proportion of the total overhead costs as part of the costs of each cost unit.

Capital expenditure – the expenditure arising when non-current (fixed) assets are purchased by an organisation. It is not charged to the income statement as an expense but is instead written off as a **depreciation charge** over the useful life of the asset.

Expenses – all business costs that are not classified as materials or labour costs.

Revenue expenditure – the expenditure incurred on 'everyday' items such as the running costs of fixed assets. It is written off in full to the income statement in the period to which it relates.

SELF TEST QUESTIONS

		Paragraph
1	Give two examples of administration expenses.	1.1
2	Give three examples of fixed and variable costs that may be incurred by the sales function.	3.3
3	Give two examples of ways in which sales invoices should be coded to enable appropriate analysis of sales income.	3.4
4	What is meant by the absorption of overhead costs or expenses?	4.3
5	Give the two most common measures of absorbing overheads on a time basis.	5.3
6	Describe why predetermined overhead absorption rates tend to be used rather than actual overhead absorption rates.	6.4
7	Give the main categories of non-production overhead.	6.8

EXAM-STYLE QUESTIONS

1 Which of the following statements is true?

A The purchase of a sales representative's car is capital expenditure and repairs to a delivery van are revenue expenditure.

B The repairs to a delivery van are capital expenditure and rent for a factory is revenue expenditure.

C The purchase of a sales representative's car is capital expenditure and purchase of computers for office use is revenue expenditure.

D The purchase of shelving for the office is capital expenditure and purchase of computers for office use is revenue expenditure.

2 The following data is available for the machining department cost centre for the latest period:

	Budget	*Actual*
Production overhead	$128,000	$132,000
Direct labour hours	25,000	25,600

What is the budgeted direct labour hour absorption rate for overheads?

A $5.00 per direct labour hour

B $5.12 per direct labour hour

C $5.16 per direct labour hour

D $5.28 per direct labour hour.

3 The following data is available for a production department cost centre for the latest period:

	Budget	Actual
Production overhead	$96,000	$108,000
Direct labour hours	25,000	26,000

What is the under/over-absorbed production overhead for the period?

A $8,160 under-absorbed

B $8,160 over-absorbed

C $12,000 under-absorbed

D $12,000 over-absorbed.

4 A cost centre has an overhead absorption rate of $4.25 per machine hour, based on a budgeted activity level of 12,400 machine hours.

In the period covered by the budget, actual machine hours worked were 2% more than the budgeted hours and the actual overhead expenditure incurred in the cost centre was $56,389.

What was the total over or under absorption of overheads in the cost centre for the period?

A $1,054 over absorbed

B $2,635 under absorbed

C $3,689 over absorbed

D $3,689 under absorbed

5 The management accountant's report shows that fixed production overheads were over-absorbed in the last accounting period.

Which combination is certain to lead to this situation?

A production volume is lower than budget and actual expenditure is higher than budget

B production volume is higher than budget and actual expenditure is higher than budget

C production volume and actual cost are as budgeted

D production volume is higher than budget and actual expenditure is lower than budget

For suggested answers, see the 'Answers' section at the end of the book.

Chapter 8

MARGINAL COSTING AND ABSORPTION COSTING

This chapter explains and compares the concepts of absorption costing and marginal costing. The chapter covers syllabus area C1(d).

CONTENTS

1   The concept of contribution

2   Absorption costing and marginal costing

3   Differences in profits under absorption costing and marginal costing

4   Absorption costing v marginal costing

5   Profit and contribution

LEARNING OUTCOMES

On completion of this chapter the student should be able to:

• Prepare, and explain the nature and purpose of, profit statements in absorption and marginal costing formats.

1 THE CONCEPT OF CONTRIBUTION

1.1 FIXED AND VARIABLE COSTS

In previous chapters a distinction was drawn between fixed costs and variable costs.

If **all** costs of a business (fixed and variable) are deducted from sales revenue, the remaining amount is known as **profit**.

1.2 CONTRIBUTION

If only the variable costs of the business are deducted from sales revenue, the resulting figure is known as contribution.

Definition   **Contribution** is sales value less **all** variable costs.

Contribution can be calculated on a per unit basis or alternatively on a total basis.

Example

A company makes and sells a single product. Details of this product are as follows:

Per unit

Selling price	$20
Direct materials	$6
Direct labour	$3
Variable overhead	$4
Fixed overhead	$20,000 per month

The fixed overhead is absorbed on the basis of expected production of 20,000 units per month.

If actual production and sales are 20,000 units in a month calculate the contribution per unit, the total contribution for the month and the total profit for the month.

Solution

Contribution per unit

	$	$
Selling price		20
Less: variable costs		
Direct materials	6	
Direct labour	3	
Variable overhead	4	
	——	13
Contribution per unit		7

Total contribution and profit

		$	$
Sales (20,000 × $20)			400,000
Variable costs:			
Direct materials	(20,000 × $6)	120,000	
Direct labour	(20,000 × $3)	60,000	
Variable overhead	($20,000 × $4)	80,000	
			260,000
Contribution			140,000
Fixed overheads			20,000
Total profit			120,000

Alternatively this could be calculated as follows:

Total contribution = Sales units × Contribution per unit (20,000 × $7) = $140,000

Less fixed costs $20,000

Profit $120,000

2 ABSORPTION COSTING AND MARGINAL COSTING

2.1 INTRODUCTION

In earlier chapters the idea of absorbing production overheads into the cost of units of production was considered in some detail. The overheads that were included in the cost of the cost units were both variable production overheads and fixed production overheads.

2.2 ABSORPTION COSTING

Definition   **Absorption costing** is a cost accounting system that charges both fixed and variable production overheads to cost units.

Under an absorption costing system each unit of inventory, whether it has been sold and charged as cost of sales or is unsold and included in closing inventory, is valued at full production cost. This includes both fixed and variable production overheads.

2.3 MARGINAL COSTING AS AN ALTERNATIVE TO ABSORPTION COSTING

Definition   **Marginal costing** is an accounting system in which variable production costs are charged to cost units and fixed production costs are not absorbed into cost units but written off in the income statement for the period to which they relate.

We saw in an earlier chapter that this involves classifying fixed production overheads as period costs and not as product costs.

Note that fixed non-production costs will always be treated as period costs.

In a marginal costing system all cost units are valued at variable production cost only.

Example

Company A produces a single product with the following budget:

Selling price	$10 per unit
Direct materials	$3 per unit
Direct wages	$2 per unit
Variable production overhead	$1 per unit
Fixed production overheads	$10,000 per month.

The fixed production overhead absorption rate is based on a production level of 5,000 units per month.

Prepare the operating statement for the month under marginal costing principles, if 4,800 units were produced and sold.

Assume that costs were as budget, and that there is no opening inventory and that there are no non-production costs.

Solution

	$
Sales (4,800 × $10)	48,000
Variable costs (4,800 × $6) (W1)	28,800
	———
Contribution (Note)	19,200
Fixed costs	10,000
	———
Profit	9,200
	———

(W1)

Variable costs = Materials ($3) + Wages ($2) + Variable overheads ($1)

= $6 per unit.

(Note)

To calculate contribution we need to deduct all variable costs – both production and non-production – from sales. Here we have only deducted variable production costs. We can only refer to this as contribution as we are told that there are no non-production costs.

2.4 MARGINAL COSTING AND INVENTORY VALUATION

Under marginal costing inventory is valued at variable production cost. This is in contrast to absorption costing where fixed production overhead costs are also included in inventory valuations using the predetermined absorption rate.

The following example illustrates the effects of the different inventory valuations on profit.

Example

Suppose that in the previous example production was in fact 6,000 units i.e. 4,800 units sold and 1,200 units left in closing inventory.

Prepare profit statements for the month using both absorption costing and marginal costing principles.

Solution

Absorption costing

With absorption costing the predetermined overhead absorption rate will be $10,000/5,000 units = $2 per unit.

Therefore the full production cost per unit for the absorption costing statement = $6 variable cost + $2 fixed production overheads = $8 per unit.

A further problem occurs because the actual level of production (6,000 units) is greater than the level of production used in calculating the overhead absorption rate (5,000 units). This leads to a situation of over-absorbed fixed production overheads, which means that more production overhead will have been absorbed into the cost of production than has been incurred during the period. This over-absorbed overhead is added back to the profit at the end of the operating statement in order to determine the absorption costing operating profit for the period.

The over-absorbed fixed production overhead is calculated as follows.

	$
Fixed production overhead absorbed (6,000 units × $2)	12,000
Fixed production overhead incurred	10,000
Over-absorbed fixed production overhead	2,000

		$	$
Sales			48,000
Cost of sales:			
Production	(6,000 × $8)	48,000	
Closing inventory	(1,200 × $8)	9,600	
			38,400
			9,600
Over-absorbed fixed overhead (see working above)			2,000
Profit			11,600

In this example there was an over absorption of fixed production overhead when absorption costing principles were used. If the actual production level had been lower than the budgeted level then there would have been an under absorption. This amount would have been deducted at the end of the statement to deduce the profit for the period.

Conclusion   Using absorption costing principles, the cost of production is valued at full production cost which includes a share of the fixed production overhead. This may mean that there is an under or over absorption of production overhead.

Marginal costing

			$	$
Sales				48,000
Variable costs:				
Production costs	(6,000 × $6)		36,000	
Closing inventory	(1,200 × $6)		7,200	
			———	28,800
				———
				19,200
Fixed costs				10,000
				———
Profit				9,200
				———

Using marginal costing principles, the cost of sales is valued at variable production cost only. The fixed production costs are written off as they are incurred as a **period cost** in the income statement. Therefore there is no absorption of fixed production overheads and consequently no under- or over-absorption.

If inventory levels increase or decrease in a period the two methods report different figures for profit.

3 DIFFERENCES IN PROFITS UNDER ABSORPTION COSTING AND MARGINAL COSTING

3.1 INTRODUCTION

As we saw in the previous example, if inventory levels increase or decrease in a period, there will be a difference in the amount of profit reported under absorption costing and marginal costing.

3.2 INVENTORY VALUATION

The only difference between absorption costing and marginal costing is the way in which inventory is valued.

Under absorption costing a share of the fixed production overhead is included in the inventory valuation whereas under marginal costing only the variable production overheads are included in the inventory valuation and all fixed production overhead is charged to the income statement. It is this different treatment of fixed production overhead that causes the difference in reported profit between the two costing systems.

If inventory levels increase then the profit under absorption costing will be higher than under marginal costing. If inventory levels fall in a period then the profit under marginal costing will be higher than under absorption costing.

The difference between the profits of two methods will always be the change in inventory multiplied by the overhead absorption rate per unit.

In the most recent example closing inventory has increased from zero to 1,200 units, so the difference in profit is 1,200 × $2 = $2,400.

In MA1 you need to be aware that the two methods can give rise to different profits but you are not expected to perform a reconciliation of the two figures.

ACTIVITY 1

A company sells a product for $10 per unit, and incurs $4 per unit of variable costs in its manufacture. The fixed production costs are $900 per year and are absorbed on the basis of the normal production volume of 250 units per year. The results for the last four years were as follows:

	1st year units	2nd year units	3rd year units	4th year units	Total units
Opening inventory	–	200	300	300	–
Production	300	250	200	200	950
	300	450	500	500	950
Closing inventory	200	300	300	200	200
Sales	100	150	200	300	750
	$	$	$	$	$
Sales value	1,000	1,500	2,000	3,000	7,500

Calculate the profit each year under both absorption costing and marginal costing.

For a suggested answer, see the 'Answers' section at the end of the book.

4 ABSORPTION COSTING v MARGINAL COSTING

4.1 ARGUMENTS FOR ABSORPTION COSTING

Absorption costing is a widely used costing method. Defenders of the absorption principle point out that:

(a) it is necessary to include fixed production overhead in inventory values for financial statements; routine cost accounting using absorption costing produces inventory values which include a share of fixed production overhead

(b) for a small jobbing business, overhead absorption is the only practicable way of obtaining job costs for estimating and profit analysis

(c) analysis of under-/over- absorbed overhead is useful for identifying inefficient utilisation of production resources.

4.2 ARGUMENTS AGAINST ABSORPTION COSTING

Preparation of routine operating statements using absorption costing is considered less informative than using marginal costing because:

(a) Profit per unit is a misleading figure: in the example the operating margin of $2 per unit arises because fixed production overhead per unit is based on 5,000 units. If another activity level were used, the profit margin per unit would differ even though the fixed production overhead cost was the same amount in total.

(b) Build-up or run-down of inventory of finished goods can distort comparison of period operating statements and obscure the effect of increasing or decreasing sales.

(c) Comparison between products can be misleading because of the effect of the arbitrary apportionment of fixed costs.

5 PROFIT AND CONTRIBUTION

5.1 INTRODUCTION

Calculations of both profit and contribution will provide managers with useful information. However each serves different purposes.

5.2 PROFIT INFORMATION

A business must make a profit in order to survive. It must ensure that in the long run all of its costs are covered. Therefore information regarding the profit that a business has made will be of great importance to management.

5.3 CONTRIBUTION INFORMATION

Contribution is sales value less variable costs. Therefore it is effectively a fund out of which firstly fixed costs are covered and then a profit is made. It is argued that contribution provides more useful information than profit particularly for decision-making purposes.

Contribution will vary directly with the level of activity as long as sales price and variable costs are constant per unit. Therefore if decisions are to be made about activity or production levels then contribution per unit will be more relevant, because the absorption costing profit per unit changes every time the activity level changes.

To determine the profitability of individual products the fixed overheads of the organisation must be apportioned in some way to each product. This apportionment is arbitrary. Therefore, when comparing products it can be argued that the contribution of each product rather than the profit will give more useful information as there is no arbitrary apportionment involved.

Conclusion   Profit information is important to management as the business must be profitable in the long run. However for most management decision purposes contribution will be more useful.

KEY TERMS

Contribution – sales value less **all** variable costs.

Absorption costing – a cost accounting system that charges both fixed and variable production costs to cost units.

Marginal costing – a cost accounting system in which only variable production costs are charged to units and fixed costs are charged to the income statement in the period to which they relate.

SELF TEST QUESTIONS

Paragraph

1   Explain the term contribution.   1.2

2   Explain what absorption costing and marginal costing methods are.   2.2, 2.3

3   How is closing inventory valued in a marginal costing system?   2.4

4   In what circumstances would there be a difference between the profit
     reported under absorption costing and the profit reported under marginal
     costing?   3.2

4   If closing inventory is greater than opening inventory will absorption
     costing profit or marginal costing profit be higher?   3.3

EXAM-STYLE QUESTIONS

1   When preparing an operating statement based on absorption costing principles,
     inventory valuation comprises which of the following costs?

     A   Direct labour and material costs only

     B   Prime cost plus variable and fixed production overhead

     C   Prime cost plus variable production overhead

     D   Total cost

2   A company manufactures and sells a single product. For this month the budgeted
     fixed production overheads are $48,000, budgeted production is 12,000 units and
     budgeted sales are 11,720 units.

     The company currently uses absorption costing.

     If the company used marginal costing principles instead of absorption costing for this
     month, what would be the effect on the budgeted profit?

     A $1,120 higher

     B $1,120 lower

     C $3,920 higher

     D $3,920 lower

3   A company has established a marginal costing profit of $72,300. Opening inventory was 300 units and closing inventory is 750 units. The fixed production overhead absorption rate has been calculated as $5/unit.

What was the profit under absorption costing?

A $67,050

B $70,050

C $74,550

D $77,550

4   In a given period, the production level of an item exactly matches the level of sales.

What would the difference in profit reported using marginal or absorption costing be?

A   The same

B   Higher under absorption costing

C   Lower under absorption costing

D   Higher under marginal costing

For suggested answers, see the 'Answers' section at the end of the book.

Chapter 9

JOB, BATCH AND PROCESS COSTING

In a manufacturing organisation, the cost unit might be a batch of output or a specific job carried out for a customer. Other businesses manufacture their output in a process operation, or a series of process operations. Each of these requires its own approach to costing.

This chapter covers syllabus areas D4(a, b and c).

CONTENTS

1   Job costing

2   Batch costing

3   Process costing

LEARNING OUTCOMES

At the end of this chapter you should be able to:

- Job costing

    (i)   Describe the characteristics of job costing.

    (ii)   Calculate unit costs using job costing.

- Batch costing

    (i)   Describe the characteristics of batch costing.

    (ii)   Calculate unit costs using batch costing.

- Process costing

    (i)   Describe the characteristics of process costing.

    (ii)   Calculate unit costs using process costing.

    (iii) Describe and illustrate the concept of equivalent units for closing WIP.

    (iv)   Calculate unit costs where there is closing work-in-progress.

    (v)   Allocate process costs between finished output and work-in-progress.

    (vi)   Prepare process accounts. .

1 JOB COSTING

1.1 JOBS

Definition   A **job** is an individual product designed and produced as a single order for an individual customer

A job will normally be requested by a customer and that customer's individual requirements and specifications considered. Each individual job is a cost unit. The organisation will then estimate the costs of such a job, add on their required profit margin and quote their price to the customer. If the customer accepts that quote then the job will proceed according to the timetable agreed between customer and supplier.

Each job will tend to be a specific individual order and as such will normally differ in some respects from other jobs that the organisation performs. The costs for each individual job must therefore be determined.

You might be able to think of organisations that perform jobbing work, and charge customers for the jobs they do. Well-known examples include small building and building repair work, car maintenance and repair work, printing, painting and decorating.

1.2 JOB COST CARD

All of the actual costs incurred in a job are eventually recorded on a job cost card. A job cost card can take many forms but is likely at least to include the following information:

JOB COST CARD	
Job number	Customer name:
Estimate ref:	Quoted estimate:
Start date:	Delivery date:
Invoice number:	Invoice amount:
COSTS:	

Materials   **Labour**
Date   Code   Qty   Price $ Date   Grade   Hours   Rate $

Expenses   **Production overheads**
Date   Code   Description $ Hours   OAR $

Cost summary:
Direct materials
Direct labour
Direct expenses
Production overheads
Administrative overheads
Selling and distribution overheads
Total cost
Invoice price

The job cost card may travel with the particular job as it moves around the factory. However it is more likely in practice that the job cost cards will be held centrally by the accounts department and all relevant cost information for that job forwarded to the accounts department.

1.3 DIRECT MATERIALS FOR JOBS

When materials are requisitioned for a job then the issue of the materials will be recorded in the inventory ledger account. They will also be recorded, at their issue price, on the job cost card as they are used as input into that particular job. Materials may be issued at different dates to a particular job but each issue must be recorded on the job cost card.

Example

The materials requisitions and issues for Job number 3867 for customer OT Ltd at their issue prices are as follows:

1 June	40 kg Material code T73 at $60 per kg
5 June	60 kg Material code R80 at $5 per kg
9 June	280 metres Material code B45 at $8 per metre

Record these on a job cost card for this job which is due to be delivered on 17 June.

Solution

JOB COST CARD										

Job number: 3867
Estimate ref:
Start date: 1 June
Invoice number:

Customer name: OT Ltd
Quoted estimate:
Delivery date: 17 June
Invoice amount:

COSTS:

Materials

Date	Code	Qty	Price	$
1 June	T73	40 kg	$60	2,400
5 June	R80	60 kg	$5	300
9 June	B45	280m	$8	2,240
				4,940

Labour

Date	Grade	Hours	Rate	$
1 June	II	43	5.80	249.4
2 June	II	12	5.80	69.6
2 June	IV	15	7.50	112.5
5	I	25	4.70	117.5
5	IV	13	7.50	97.5
5	I	15/123	4.70	70.5
				717

Expenses

Date	Code	Description	$

Production overheads

Hours	OAR	$

Cost summary:

	$
Direct materials	4940
Direct labour	717
Direct expenses	400
Production overheads	492
Administration overheads	156
Selling and distribution overheads	78
Total cost	6783
Invoice price	7,800
Profit/loss	1017

1.4 DIRECT LABOUR COST FOR JOBS

In an earlier chapter dealing with labour costs the system of recording hours worked in a job costing system was considered.

In summary a job card travels with each individual job and the hours worked by each grade of labour are logged onto this card. The card is then sent to the accounts department and the hours are transferred to the job cost card. The relevant hourly labour rate is then applied to each grade of labour to give a cost for each grade and a total cost for the job.

ACTIVITY 1

The labour records show that the hours worked on Job 3867 were as follows:

1 June	Grade II	43 hours
2 June	Grade II	12 hours
	Grade IV	15 hours
5 June	Grade I	25 hours
	Grade IV	13 hours
9 June	Grade I	15 hours

The hourly rates for each grade of labour are as follows:

	$
Grade I	4.70
Grade II	5.80
Grade III	6.40
Grade IV	7.50

Record the labour costs for Job 3867 on the job cost card.

For a suggested answer, see the 'Answers' section at the end of the book.

1.5 DIRECT EXPENSES

The third category of direct costs are any expenses that can be directly attributed to that particular job. Such expenses will be recorded by the cost accountant when incurred and coded in such a way that it is clear to which job or jobs they relate.

ACTIVITY 2

A specialised piece of machinery has been hired at a cost of $1,200. It is used on job numbers 3859, 3867 and 3874 and has spent approximately the same amount of time being used on each of those jobs. The account code for machine hire is 85.

Record any cost relevant to Job 3867 on the job cost card.

For a suggested answer, see the 'Answers' section at the end of the book.

KAPLAN PUBLISHING

1.6   PRODUCTION OVERHEADS AND JOB COSTS

In an earlier chapter the apportionment of overheads to cost units was considered and it was determined that the most common method of allocating overheads to specific cost units was on the basis of either the labour hours worked or machine hours worked on that particular cost unit.

This is exactly the same for jobs and so the production overhead will be absorbed into jobs on the basis of the pre-determined overhead absorption rate.

1.7   OTHER OVERHEADS AND JOB COSTS

In order to arrive at the total cost for a particular job any administration, selling and distribution overheads must also be included in the job's cost. Therefore when the job is completed an appropriate proportion of the total administration, selling and distribution overheads will also be included on the job cost card.

ACTIVITY 3

The production overhead absorption rate for this period is $4 per labour hour. The administration overhead to be charged to Job 3867 totals $156 and the selling and distribution overhead for the job is $78.

The job was completed by the due date and the customer was invoiced the agreed price of $7,800 on 17 June (invoice number 26457).

Using this information complete the job cost card for Job 3867.

For a suggested answer, see the 'Answers' section at the end of the book.

2   BATCH COSTING

The second type of costing system that must be examined is a batch costing system. A batch costing system is likely to be very similar to a job costing system and indeed a batch is in all respects a job.

2.1   BATCH

Definition   A **batch** is a group of identical but separately identifiable products that are all made together.

A batch is for example a group of 100 identical products made in a particular production run. For example, a baker may produce loaves of bread in batches.

2.2   BATCH COSTING

Each batch is very similar to a job and in exactly the same way as in job costing the costs of that batch are gathered together on some sort of a batch cost card. These costs will be the materials input into the batch, the labour worked on the batch, any direct expenses of the batch and the batch's share of overheads.

The layout of the batch cost card will be similar to that of a job cost card. This will show the total cost of that particular batch of production.

2.3 COST OF A COST UNIT

Remember that a batch does however differ from a job in that a batch is made up of a number of identical products or cost units. In order to find the cost of each product or cost unit the total cost of the batch must be divided by the number of products in that batch.

Example

Batch number 0692 has the following inputs:

15 June Material X   20 kg @ $30 per kg

40 hours of grade II labour @ $6.00 per hour

16 June Material Y   15 kg @ $10 per kg

60 hours of grade III labour at $5.00 per hour

Production overhead is to be absorbed into the cost of each batch on the basis of labour hours at a rate of $0.50 per labour hour.

The number of products produced from batch 0692 was 100.

Calculate the cost of each product from batch 0692.

Solution

Materials cost	$
Material X 20 kg × $30	600
Material Y 15 kg × $10	150
Labour cost	
Grade II 40 hours × $6	240
Grade III 60 hours × $5	300
Production overhead	
100 hours × $0.50	50
	———
	1,340
	———

Cost per cost unit or product

$$\frac{\$1,340}{100\,\text{units}} = \$13.40$$

3 PROCESS COSTING

3.1 INTRODUCTION

Process costing is the costing method applicable where goods or services result from a sequence of continuous or repetitive operations or processes. Process costing is used when a company is mass producing the same item and the item goes through a number of different stages.

Process costing is sometimes referred to as continuous operation costing.

Examples include the chemical, cement, oil, paint and textile industries.

Two key issues that complicate process costing are losses and incomplete units at the end of the period. These are discussed below.

3.2 ILLUSTRATION OF PROCESS COSTING

Here is an example of a two-process manufacturing operation:

HYRA has a manufacturing operation that involves two processes. The data for the first process during a particular period is as follows:

- At the beginning of the period, 2,500 kg materials are introduced to the process at a cost of $3,500.

- These materials are then worked upon, using $600 of labour and incurring/absorbing $450 of overheads.

The resulting output is passed to the second process.

To keep track of the costs we could prepare a process account for each process. This resembles a T account with extra columns. The reason for the extra columns is that we have to keep track of how many units we are working on as well as their value.

The costs appearing in such an account are those for materials, labour and overheads. (Labour and overheads are often combined under the heading 'conversion costs'.) In the case of materials we record both units and monetary amount; in the case of conversion costs we record the monetary amount only, because they do not add any units.

With process accounts the inputs into the process go into the left (debit) side of the account and output on the right (credit) side.

The process account for the above example might thus appear as follows.

Process 1 account

	Kg	$		Kg	$
Materials	2,500	3,500	Output		
Labour		600	materials to		
Overheads *o/h*		450	Process 2	2,500	4,550
	2,500	4,550		2,500	4,550

Conversion { Labour, Overheads

3.3 THE BASIC PROCESS COST PER UNIT

Process costing is very similar to batch costing, as we calculate the total costs for the process and divide by the number of units to get a cost per unit.

The main difference is that the process is ongoing so the costs and output for a particular time period are used.

Using the example above we can calculate the cost per kg of output that will be transferred to the second process:

The calculation that needs to be done:

$$\text{Cost per unit} = \frac{\text{Net costs of input}}{\text{Output}}$$

Net costs of input = $3,500 + $600 + $450 = $4,550

Output = 2,500 kg

Thus, the output to process 2 would be costed at:

$$\frac{\$4,550}{2,500 \text{ kg}} = \$1.82 \text{ per kg output}$$

3.4 LOSSES

In many industrial processes, some input is lost (through evaporation, wastage, etc) or damaged during the production process. This will give rise to losses in the process. We will look at the concepts of normal losses and abnormal losses or gains.

Expected loss   *unexpected. loss*

Normal loss represents items that you expect to lose during a process, and its cost is therefore treated as part of the cost of good production. Abnormal losses or gains are not expected so are valued at the same cost as good production.

In exam questions you are not expected to have to split losses into normal and abnormal.

Normal losses are usually stated as a percentage of input i.e. the normal loss is expected to be 5% of the input material. Unless the normal loss can be sold as scrap the cost of the loss is absorbed into the production cost.

Illustration

At the start of a heating process 1,000 kg of material costing $16 per kg is input. During the process, conversion costs of $2,000 are incurred. Normal loss (through evaporation) is expected to be 10% of input. During March 1,000 kg were input and output was 900 kg.

Compute the unit and total cost of output in March.

Solution

First we need to sort out the units. We can do this using the flow of units equation:

Input	=>	Output	+	Loss
1,000 kg	=>	900 kg	+	100 kg (to balance)

The normal loss is 10% of input = 100 kg thus the loss was as expected i.e. it is all normal loss.

We now need to compute the cost per unit of good output

Total input costs:

Materials	$16 × 1,000 kg	$16,000
Conversion costs		$2,000
		$18,000

These costs will be spread over the expected output units – thus the cost attributable to the normal loss units is absorbed into the good units.

Cost per unit of output:

$$= \frac{\text{Net costs of input}}{\text{Expected good output}} = \frac{\$18,000}{(1,000 - 100)} = \$20 \text{ per kg}$$

Where the expected output is the input units less the normal loss units

Total cost of output = 900 kg × $20 = $18,000.

This can be represented in a process account as follows.

Process account – March

	Kg	$		Kg	$
Input	1,000	16,000	Output	900	18,000
Conversion costs	–	2,000	Normal loss	100	–
	1,000	18,000		1,000	18,000

Notice that the units and the monetary amounts balance. Normal loss is valued at zero as its cost has been absorbed into that of good output.

3.5 EQUIVALENT UNITS

Process costing is also used when products may not be completed at the end of a time period (e.g. manufacturing cars). This means that the process costs are shared between finished or complete units and work in progress or partially completed units.

We need to decide how the costs should be split over these different categories of production.

To be able to assign the correct amount of cost to finished and partially completed units of product we use a concept called Equivalent Units or EU. To demonstrate this concept:

If we had 1,000 units that are 50% complete at the end of a period. How many finished units is this equivalent to?

1,000 × 50% = 500 equivalent units (EU).

In other words, we assume we could have made 500 units and finished them instead of half finishing 1,000 units.

The calculation of equivalent units:

Equivalent units = Number of physical units × percentage completion

Illustration

EM Ltd is a manufacturer. In Period 1 the following production occurred.

Started	=	1,400 units
Closing work-in-progress (abbreviated as CWIP)	=	400 units

Degree of completion of CWIP:

Materials	100%
Conversion	50%

Costs incurred in Period 1:

Materials	$81,060
Conversion	$71,940

Solution

Started	= >	Finished	+	CWIP
1,400	= >	1,000 (to balance)	+	400

Finished units are 100% complete for both material and conversion.

		EUs
Materials	– Finished 1,000 ×100%	1,000
	– CWIP 400 × 100%	400
Conversion	– Finished 1,000 × 100%	1,000
	– CWIP 400 × 50%	200

Put the EU and costs into the table below:

Input	Equivalent units			Costs	Costs per EU ($)
	Completed in period EU	CWIP EU	Total EU	Total costs ($)	
Materials	1,000	400 (100%)	1,400	81,060	57.90
Conversion	1,000	200 (50%)	1,200	71,940	59.95
				153,000	**117.85**

Total costs are then divided by the total EU to get a cost per EU for each type of input cost, and a total cost for each completed unit.

The costs may now be attributed to the categories of output as follows:

		$	$
Completed units:	1,000 × $117.85		117,850
Closing WIP:	Materials 400 × $57.90	23,160	
	Conversion 200 × $59.95	11,990	
			35,150
			153,000

The process account would appear as follows:

Process account

	$		$
Materials	81,060	Completed goods	117,850
Conversion	71,940	Closing WIP	35,150
	153,000		153,000

Note that the treatment of equivalent units for opening WIP is outside the MA1 syllabus.

ACTIVITY 4

On 1 March 20X0 a process started work on 350 units and at the end of the month there were still 75 units in the process, each 60% complete. The process has costs so far of $3,696.

Required

The value of the finished goods and CWIP is:

	Finished goods	CWIP
A	$3,176.25	$866.25
B	$1,155	$2,541
C	$3,176.25	$519.75
D	$1,155	$4,235

For a suggested answer, see the 'Answers' section at the end of the book.

ACTIVITY 5

Egton Farm Supplies Ltd produce fertilisers and chemicals. One of its products 'Eg3' is produced in a single process.

The following information relates to period 5, 20X1.

Inputs:	Direct material	1,000 tonnes of 'X' at $70/tonne.
	Direct labour	60 hours at $8/hour.
	Overhead recovery rate	$4/hour.
Completed output:		800 tonnes
Closing work-in-progress:		200 tonnes

There were no losses in the process.

Work-in-progress degree of completion

Material	100%
Labour	80%
Overhead	80%

Prepare the process account for period 5

For a suggested answer, see the 'Answers' section at the end of the book.

CONCLUSION

Job and batch costing are costing systems used to determine the full cost of a specific job or batch of products or services. A profit mark-up may be added to arrive at a price which can be quoted to the customer. This price is often a fixed price and it is important that costs do not exceed their forecast level otherwise profit levels will be much lower than expected.

Process costing is a form of absorption costing used in processing industries. One key feature of process costing is that any expected losses are not given any cost or value, except for any scrap value they might have, and costs per unit are calculated on the basis of expected output. If actual output differs from expected output, there is abnormal loss or abnormal gain, which are given a cost/value.

A second feature of process costing is that process costs have to be apportioned between finished output and closing inventory. The apportionment of costs is on the basis of equivalent units of work done.

KEY TERMS

Job – an individual product designed and produced as a single order for an individual customer.

Batch – a group of identical but separately identifiable products that are all made together.

Costs of conversion – the labour costs of the process plus the overheads of the process.

Normal loss – expected amounts of loss in a production process. It is the level of loss or waste that management would expect to incur under normal operating conditions.

Equivalent units – used to value units of incomplete work-in-process, the equivalent of one complete unit.

SELF TEST QUESTIONS

Paragraph

1	What is job costing?	1.1
2	What does a job cost card look like?	1.2
3	How is labour cost included on a job cost card?	1.4
4	How are production overheads dealt with in job costing?	1.6
5	What is batch costing?	2.1
6	Define the term normal loss.	3.4
7	Work-in-progress valuation is based on which concept?	3.5

EXAM-STYLE QUESTIONS

1   A job requires 2,400 actual labour hours for completion and it is anticipated that there will be 20% idle time.

If the wage rate is $10 per hour, what is the budgeted labour cost for the job?

A $19,200

B $24,000

C $28,800

D $30,000

2   The following items may be used in costing jobs in an absorption costing system:

(i)   actual material cost

(ii)   actual manufacturing overheads

(iii) absorbed manufacturing overheads

(iv)   actual labour cost.

Which of the above are contained in a typical job cost?

A   (i), (ii) and (iv) only

B   (i) and (iv) only

C   (i), (iii) and (iv) only

D   All four of them

3 Which one of the following statements is *incorrect*?

    A   Job costs are collected separately for each job, whereas process costs are averages based on equivalent units.

    B   A garage is more likely to use job costing for car repairs than process costing.

    C   In process costing information is needed about work passing through a process and work remaining in each process.

    D   In process costing, but not job costing, the cost of normal loss will be incorporated into normal product costs.

4 Process B had no opening WIP. 13,500 units' worth of raw material were transferred in at $4.50 per unit. Additional overheads at $1.25 per unit were added in the process. Labour costs were $6.25 per completed unit and $2.50 per unit incomplete.

If 11,750 completed units were transferred out, what was the value of closing WIP in Process B?

    A $77,625.00

    B $14,437.50

    C $141,000.00

    D $21,000.00

5 Glasgow Inc has started a new process assembling window frames. In the first month 2,000 frames were started and at the end of the month 1,700 had been finished. Of those not finished 50% of the materials had been incorporated and 30% of the labour and overhead needed had been incurred. Materials cost for the period were $5,550 and for labour and overhead were $4,475.

What was the value of the closing work-in-progress?

    A $675

    B $720

    C $825

    D $940

6 In process costing, which of the following is the best description of an equivalent unit?

    A   a notional whole unit representing incomplete work

    B   a unit made at standard performance

    C   a unit being currently made which is the same as previously manufactured

    D   a unit made in more than one process cost centre

For the answers to these questions; see the 'Answers' section at the end of the book.

Chapter 10

PERFORMANCE INDICATORS

In this chapter we will be dealing with a range of different performance indicators. The chapter covers syllabus areas C2(e and f).

CONTENTS

1   Performance measures

2   Measuring cost centre performance

3   Measuring profit centre performance

4   Measuring investment centre performance

LEARNING OUTCOMES

On completion of this chapter the student should be able to:

- Describe performance measures appropriate to cost, profit and investment centres

- Apply performance measures appropriate to cost, profit and investment centres.

1 PERFORMANCE MEASURES

1.1 INTRODUCTION

In this chapter we will examine a variety of performance indicators. Performance indicators provide information to management as to how the business is operating. There is a huge range of such indicators, made up of financial information, non-financial information or a mixture of the two.

1.2 PERFORMANCE MEASURES APPROPRIATE TO RESPONSIBILITY CENTRES

We have already seen that the different types of responsibility centre are cost centres, profit centres and investment centres. The manager responsible for the performance of each of these types of centre will be able to exercise control over different aspects of the centre's operations. It is important that a performance measure used to monitor the performance of the centre is appropriate to the type of centre, in that it monitors aspects of the centre's performance over which the manager can exercise some control.

2 MEASURING COST CENTRE PERFORMANCE

The manager of a cost centre is able to control only the costs incurred in the centre. As such, performance measures will focus on costs, productivity and quality.

2.1 CONTROLLABLE AND UNCONTROLLABLE COSTS

The manager of a cost centre may not be able to control all the costs incurred in the centre. In this context is important to distinguish between controllable costs and non-controllable costs.

A **controllable cost** is one over which a particular manager can exercise some influence, for example the cost of direct labour in a production cost centre is usually controllable by the manager of that cost centre.

A **non-controllable cost** is one which cannot be influenced by a particular manager. For example the rent of the whole factory would not be controllable by the manager of a production cost centre. It would not be fair and it could cause motivation problems if the manager was held responsible for this cost over which he is not able to exercise any control.

Note that a cost which is non-controllable for one manager will be classified as controllable for another manager. For example the factory rent will be non-controllable for the manager of a particular production cost centre but the rent is likely to be classified as a controllable cost for the general manager who has overall responsibility for the whole factory.

A cost centre manager can be monitored according to costs incurred and according to the resources utilised. For example the productivity ratios considered earlier in this chapter would be appropriate for monitoring the efficiency of a production cost centre.

The absolute amount of cost incurred in a cost centre might be a useful control measure but if output can be measured then cost per unit might be more informative.

Example: cost per unit

Department A incurred the following labour costs and produced the following output in the latest two periods:

	Period 1	Period 2
Labour costs	$96,800	$99,700
Units produced	9,500	9,920

Calculate the labour cost per unit in each period and comment on the result.

Solution

Period 1	labour cost per unit	=	$96,800/9,500	=	$10.19
Period 2	labour cost per unit	=	$99,700/9,920	=	$10.05

Although the total labour cost incurred in department A increased in period 2, the output also increased but by proportionately more. Therefore the labour cost per unit reduced in period 2 compared with period 1.

2.2 PRODUCTIVITY MEASURES

A **productivity measure** relates the goods or services produced to the resources used to produce them. The most productive or efficient operations produce the maximum output from given resource inputs or alternatively, use the minimum inputs for any given quantity or quality of output.

Note:

It is important to be able to distinguish between production and productivity.

Production is the quantity of goods or services that are produced. Productivity is a measure of how efficiently those goods or services have been produced.

Production levels are reasonably straightforward for management to control as they can be increased by working more hours or taking on more employees, or decreased by cutting overtime or laying off employees. Production levels can also be increased by increasing productivity and vice versa.

Productivity however, is perhaps more difficult for management to control as it can only be increased by producing more goods or services with a given set of resources, or alternatively, reaching set production targets using less resources.

2.3 STANDARD HOURS

Before we look at productivity ratios we need to define what is known as a **standard hour**.

Definition The standard hour is defined as 'the amount of work achievable in an hour'.

A standard hour is calculated as:

$$\frac{\text{Budgeted output}}{\text{Budgeted production hours}}$$

Example

The budgeted output for a period is 400 units and the budgeted time for the production of these units is 200 hours.

The standard hour = 400/200 = 2 units per hour

Equivalently we could state that the budget is based on the assumption that each unit takes half an hour (30 minutes) to make.

This information is very useful for comparing output in different periods or against budget.

Example

Briggs plc set its budget for the coming month as follows:

- Standard hour = 4 units

- Budgeted hours = 300 hours

- Budgeted output = 300 × 4 = 1,200 units

The actual output in May was 1,100 units that were produced in 250 hours.

How did the production manager perform?

At first sight we might suggest that performance was poor due to a fall in production. However, there are two issues here:

- For some reason, only 250 hours were worked. We are not told why this was lower than budgeted.

- In that time actually worked we would have expected output of 250 × 4 = 1,000 units. The production department produced 100 more units than expected, so should be commended.

This type of analysis can be developed further through the use of productivity ratios.

2.4 PRODUCTIVITY RATIOS

Productivity is often analysed using three labour control ratios:

- production volume or activity ratio

- capacity utilisation ratio

- efficiency or productivity ratio

Example

The budgeted output for a period is 2,000 units and the budgeted time for the production of these units is 200 hours.

The actual output in the period is 2,300 units and the actual time worked by the labour force is 180 hours.

Calculate the production volume, capacity utilisation and efficiency ratios.

2.5 PRODUCTION VOLUME RATIO

Definition The **production volume ratio** assesses the overall production. Over 100% indicates that overall production is above planned levels and below 100% indicates a shortfall compared to plans.

The production volume ratio is calculated as:

$$\frac{\text{Actual output measured in standard hours}}{\text{Budgeted production hours}} \times 100\%$$

Solution – production volume ratio

Standard hour	=	$\dfrac{2{,}000 \text{ units}}{200 \text{ hours}}$
	=	10 units
Actual output measured in standard hours	=	$\dfrac{2{,}300 \text{ units}}{10 \text{ units}}$
	=	230 standard hours
Production volume ratio	=	$\dfrac{230}{200} \times 100\%$
	=	115%

This shows that production is 15% higher than the planned production levels.

2.6 CAPACITY UTILISATION RATIO

Definition The **capacity utilisation ratio** indicates worker capacity, in terms of the hours of working time that have been possible in a period.

The capacity utilisation ratio is calculated as:

$$\text{Capacity utilisation ratio} = \frac{\text{Actual hours worked}}{\text{Budgeted hours}} \times 100\%$$

Solution – capacity utilisation ratio

$$\text{Capacity utilisation ratio} = \frac{180 \text{ hours}}{200 \text{ hours}} = 90\%$$

Therefore this organisation had only 90% of the budgeted labour hours for production.

2.7 EFFICIENCY RATIO

Definition The **efficiency ratio** is an indicator of productivity with the benchmark being 100%.

The efficiency ratio is calculated as follows:

$$\frac{\text{Actual output measured in standard hours}}{\text{Actual hours worked}}$$

The efficiency ratio is often referred to as the productivity ratio.

Solution – efficiency ratio

$$\text{Efficiency ratio} \quad = \quad \frac{230}{180} \times 100\% \quad = \quad 127.78\%$$

This can be proved. The workers were expected to produce 10 units per hour, the standard hour. Therefore, in the 180 hours worked it would be expected that 1,800 units would be produced. In fact 2,300 units were produced. This is 27.78% more than anticipated (500/1,800).

2.8   RATIO RELATIONSHIPS

The three ratios calculated above can be summarised diagrammatically as follows:

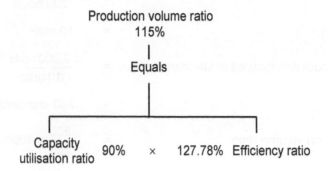

Conclusion

Note the difference between production and productivity. Production is output in terms of units e.g. 1,000 units per month. Productivity is this output expressed relative to a vital resource e.g. 10 cars per employee per year or 12 tons of steel per employee per month.

The efficiency or productivity ratio measures the productivity of the labour force in comparison to 100%. If the productivity ratio is higher than 100% then this indicates higher than anticipated productivity and if it is lower than 100%, lower than anticipated productivity.

ACTIVITY 1

Using the Briggs plc example introduced above:

• Standard hour = 4 units

• Budgeted hours = 300 hours

• Budgeted output = 300 × 4 = 1,200 units

• The actual output in May was 1,100 units that were produced in 250 hours.

Calculate the following labour ratios and explain their meaning:

• production volume ratio

• capacity utilisation ratio

• efficiency ratio.

For a suggested answer, see the 'Answers' section at the end of the book.

2.9 QUALITY MEASURES

As well as monitoring costs and productivity, the manager of a cost centre would also want to ensure that quality standards are not compromised. Typical quality related performance measures could include the following:

- % of raw materials and components that are rejected as part of regular quality control testing of items delivered by suppliers

- % of finished items that are rejected as part of regular quality control testing of items delivered by suppliers.

3 MEASURING PROFIT CENTRE PERFORMANCE

3.1 COST CENTRE MEASURES REVISITED

The manager of a profit centre has control over the revenues earned as well as the costs incurred, therefore all the performance measures mentioned for cost centres would also apply to a profit centre.

3.2 QUALITY MEASURES EXTENDED

In addition to the quality measures discussed above, a profit centre will most likely have external customers so can have additional quality measures linked to these:

- % of items sold that are rejected by customers and returned

- % of items sold that require additional work under guarantees or warrantees

- Results of customer satisfaction surveys.

3.3 PROFIT MEASURES

In addition to the measures above, performance measures based on profit would also be appropriate for a profit centre.

The following example will demonstrate a range of performance measures that might be used to monitor a profit centre's performance.

Example: monitoring profit centre performance

Profit Centre A achieved the following results in the latest periods.

	Period 5	Period 6
Units produced	2,300	2,600
	$	$
Sales value of output	27,600	31,400
Direct costs	18,400	21,820
Overheads	5,300	3,950
	23,700	25,770
Profit	3,900	5,630

Comment on Profit Centre A's performance.

Solution

Profit margin

The profit margin calculates the profit achieved as a percentage of sales value.

$$\text{Profit margin} = \frac{\text{Profit}}{\text{Sales}} \times 100\%$$

$$\text{Period 5} = \frac{3,900}{27,600} \times 100\% = 14.1\%$$

$$\text{Period 6} = \frac{5,630}{31,400} \times 100\% = 17.9\%$$

The profit margin has improved, indicating that more profit has been earned per $1 of sales revenue generated.

Cost to sales ratio

Looking at the ratios of costs incurred to sales value achieved can help to provide more information for cost control to improve profitability.

$$\text{Direct cost percentage} = \frac{\text{Direct cost}}{\text{Sales}} \times 100\%$$

$$\text{Period 5} = \frac{18,400}{27,600} \times 100\% = 66.7\%$$

$$\text{Period 6} = \frac{21,820}{31,400} \times 100\% = 69.5\%$$

$$\text{Overhead cost percentage} = \frac{\text{Overheads}}{\text{Sales}} \times 100\%$$

$$\text{Period 5} = \frac{5,300}{27,600} \times 100\% = 19.2\%$$

$$\text{Period 6} = \frac{3,950}{31,400} \times 100\% = 12.6\%$$

Control of overhead costs was good but profitability would have been improved if the direct cost percentage had been maintained at period 5 levels.

Profit per unit

The profit per unit can only be calculated if all units produced are identical. Otherwise it would be necessary to express the output in terms of standard hours produced.

Profit per unit:

$$\text{Period 5} = \frac{\$3,900}{2,300} = \$1.70$$

$$\text{Period 6} = \frac{\$5,630}{2,600} = \$2.17$$

Improvement in the profit margin has led to a substantial increase in the profit earned per unit sold.

4 MEASURING INVESTMENT CENTRE PERFORMANCE

4.1 COST AND PROFIT CENTRE MEASURES REVISITED

The manager of an investment centre has control over costs and revenues and over the level of investment in the centre, therefore all the performance measures mentioned for both cost and profit centres would also apply to an investment centre.

In addition investment centres can use performance measures that relate the profit earned to the level of investment in the centre. The most important measures that you need to know about are **return on capital employed, residual income** and **asset turnover**.

4.2 RETURN ON CAPITAL EMPLOYED (ROCE)

ROCE is also referred to as Return on Investment (ROI). There are several ways of measuring ROCE/ROI but the profit figure normally used is the profit before interest and tax.

$$ROCE = \frac{\text{Profit before interest and tax}}{\text{Capital employed}} \times 100\%$$

Capital employed is a sum of non-current (fixed) assets and net current assets.

Although it is better to base the calculation on average capital employed during the year, the calculation is often based on year-end capital employed.

Example: calculating ROCE

Division X achieved the following results for the latest two periods.

	Period 1 $	Period 2 $
Profit before interest and tax	55,800	67,200
Capital employed	329,000	373,300

$$\text{Period 1 ROCE} = \frac{55,800}{329,000} \times 100\% = 17.0\%$$

$$\text{Period 2 ROCE} = \frac{67,200}{373,300} \times 100\% = 18.0\%$$

The division's performance improved in period 2 compared with period 1 because more profit was earned per $1 of capital invested in the division.

4.3 RESIDUAL INCOME (RI)

Alternatively a residual income approach could be used where the profit is measured as the surplus available after deducting a notional figure for interest on the capital employed in the investment centre.

Residual income (RI) = Investment centre profit − Notional interest on capital employed in centre

Example: calculating residual income (RI)

Using the data from the ROCE example above, and assuming a notional interest charge of 12% each period, the residual income is calculated as follows.

Period 1 residual income = $55,800 – ($329,000 × 12%) = $16,320

Period 2 residual income = $67,200 – ($373,300 × 12%) = $22,404

A positive RI was earned in both periods, because the ROCE was greater than the 12% notional interest cost. RI was greatly improved in period 2 because a higher return was earned on a greater amount of capital invested in the division.

Controllable and non-controllable items

When measuring the ROCE or RI of an investment centre it is important to monitor performance based on only the controllable items. Only controllable revenues and costs should be attributed to the investment centre, and only those capital employed items over which the centre manager can exercise control must be included.

For example, if the manager has discretion over the level of inventory held, then inventory values must be included in the capital employed figure. However, if the investment centre manager does not have control over the company's credit policy, then receivables should be excluded from the capital employed figure.

4.4 ASSET TURNOVER RATIO

The asset turnover ratio measures how efficiently the assets of an organisation are used to generate revenue.

$$\text{Asset turnover ratio} = \frac{\text{Revenue}}{\text{Capital employed}}$$

Example: calculating asset turnover

The following data relates to company A and company B.

	Company A $	Company B $
Revenue	800,000	600,000
Capital employed	400,000	400,000

$$\textbf{Asset turnover company A} = \frac{800,000}{400,000} = 2$$

$$\textbf{Asset turnover company B} = \frac{600,000}{400,000} = 1.5$$

Asset turnover is expressed as 'x times'. Therefore, the asset turnover for company A shows that capital employed ($400,000) generates 2 times its value in revenue ($800,000). Company B has the same capital employed ($800,000), but only generates 1.5 times the value of these assets in revenue ($600,000).

4.5   THE LINK BETWEEN PROFIT MARGIN, ASSET TURNOVER AND ROCE

The return on capital employed can also be calculated using known results for profit margin and asset turnover as follows:

ROCE = Profit margin × Asset turnover

Similarly, if only ROCE and asset turnover are known, the profit margin can be calculated by rearranging the equation above:

$$\text{Profit margin} = \frac{\text{ROCE}}{\text{Asset turnover}} \quad \text{or Asset turnover} = \frac{\text{ROCE}}{\text{Profit margin}}$$

ACTIVITY 2

The following results are available for divisions A and B.

	Division A	Division B
	$	$
Revenue	160,050	252,000
Profit	15,800	27,300
Capital employed	106,700	210,000

Calculate the following for each division and comment on the results:

(a)   ROCE

(b)   residual income, using a notional interest rate of 11% per period

(c)   asset turnover ratio.

For a suggested answer, see the 'Answers' section at the end of the book.

CONCLUSION

Management compare data to produce useful information for planning, control and decision-making purposes.

KEY TERMS

Productivity measure – relates the goods or services produced to the resources used to produce them. The most productive or efficient operation produces the maximum output from given resource inputs or, alternatively, uses the minimum inputs for any given quantity or quality of output.

$$\text{Production volume ratio} = \frac{\text{Actual output measured in standard hours}}{\text{Budgeted production hours}} \times 100\%$$

$$\text{Capacity utilisation ratio} = \frac{\text{Actual hours worked}}{\text{Budgeted hours}} \times 100\%$$

$$\text{Efficiency ratio} = \frac{\text{Actual output measured in standard hours}}{\text{Actual hours worked}}$$

Resource utilisation – a measure of how an organisation uses its inputs or resources.

Residual income – surplus profit after charging a notional interest charge for use of net assets (or capital) employed.

ROCE – return on capital employed. It measures the profit earned as a percentage of the capital employed.

Asset turnover – a measure of how efficiently the assets of an organisation are used to generate revenue.

SELF TEST QUESTIONS

		Paragraph
1	What is a productivity measure?	1.2
2	What does the capacity utilisation ratio measure?	1.6
3	What is the ROCE ratio?	2.3
4	How is residual income calculated?	2.3
5	What does the asset turnover ratio measure?	2.3

EXAM-STYLE QUESTIONS

1   Which of the following performance measures would not be suitable for a cost centre?

    A   Direct cost per employee

    B   Profit margin

    C   Overhead cost per machine hour

    D   Productivity ratio

2   The following results are available for Division Y:

Profit before interest and tax	$185,000
Capital employed	$1,540,000

    The cost of capital is 10%.

    What is the ROCE for Division Y?

    A $18,500

    B   12%

    C $31,000

    D   10%

3   Which of the following statements are true or false?

		True	False
(a)	A production volume ratio of 110% means that overall production is 10% higher than planned levels.	✓	
(b)	A capacity utilisation ratio of 95% means that actual hours of production are 5% less than planned.	✓	
(c)	An efficiency ratio of 105% means that 5% more units were produced than planned.		✓

For suggested answers, see the 'Answers' section at the end of the book.

Chapter 11

SPREADSHEETS

Modern accountants make widespread use of software and information technology. A key element of this is the use of spreadsheets. Spreadsheets can simplify and speed up many accounting tasks. This chapter aims to explain the benefits of spreadsheets, their practical uses and how they can be used to display information. This chapter covers syllabus areas E1 to E3.

CONTENTS

LEARNING OUTCOMES

At the end of this chapter you should be able to:

- Explain the purposes of a spreadsheet.

- Describe the components of a blank spreadsheet screen.

- Describe methods to use/activate spreadsheet features.

- Describe methods of selecting ranges of cells.

- Explain the role of spreadsheets in management accounting.

- Describe the advantages and limitations of spreadsheets.

- Explain factors that influence spreadsheet design and the features of a well-structured worksheet/workbook.

- Explain how to enter values, text and dates including automatically filling a range of cells and capturing data from another source.

- Identify and use formulae incorporating common arithmetic operators, use of brackets, absolute/relative cell references and simple functions (Sum, Average, Round, IF)

- Identify and use formulae in a workbook containing multiple worksheets and link cells from different workbooks.

- Describe how to move/copy and paste data and formulae.

- Describe, and select as appropriate, ways to edit data in a cell including the Find and Replace feature.

- Explain the causes of common error messages and how errors are corrected.

- Describe how to save, password protect and open spreadsheets

- Describe and illustrate appropriate formatting features for the display of numbers, text, cell borders and patterns and for cell/worksheet protection.

- Describe features that can be applied to rows or columns (changing height/width, inserting, deleting and hiding).

- Describe features that affect the on screen view and can be particularly useful when working with large worksheets/workbooks.

- Use Sort and Filter to manipulate data.

- Describe how charts (line, bar, pie, scatter, area) can be created from spreadsheet data and interpret the data shown.

- Describe and illustrate the appropriate use of adding comments to a cell.

- Describe how to select the output to be printed

- Select the combination of page layout/set-up options to achieve an effective, user-friendly printed output, especially for worksheets containing large amounts of data.

1 SPREADSHEETS OVERVIEW

1.1 SPREADSHEETS

A spreadsheet is a computer program that allows numbers to be entered and manipulated. The numbers can be presented with text, and there is usually a facility to provide a visual analysis of numbers with graphs and charts.

Essentially, a spreadsheet is a huge table of rows and columns, with columns given letters (A to Z followed by AA to AZ and so on) and rows numbered sequentially. Columns and rows are marked by vertical and horizontal lines, so that a blank spreadsheet looks like a large table of empty boxes. Each box or cell has a unique identification reference (e.g. cell D7 is in column D and row 7).

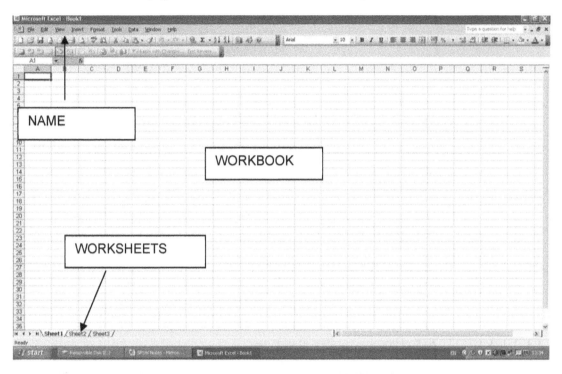

A spreadsheet has been described as a giant calculator. A large amount of information can be entered in the cells. Each cell might contain text, or a number or a formula. When a formula is entered in a cell, the program automatically carries out a calculation on numbers in one or more other cells, and shows the answer in the formula cell.

A spreadsheet is used to manipulate data. The word **spreadsheet** has its origins in the large sheets of paper used by accountants, over which they spread their figures and calculations in neat rows and columns. The little boxes made by the horizontal and vertical lines have their counterpart in the PC's spreadsheet and are called **cells**.

Into these cells may be entered numbers, text or a **formula**. Formulae are not visible when the user is entering data but reside in the background. A formula normally involves a mathematical calculation on the content of other cells, the result being inserted in the cell containing the formula.

The size of spreadsheets, in terms of the number of columns and rows, varies greatly between packages. Spreadsheets with millions of cells are possible. Because most business worksheets are quite large, extending beyond the edge of the computer screen, the screen is in effect a 'window' into the worksheet. Some or all of the spreadsheet can be printed out directly or saved on disk for insertion into reports or other documents using a word processing package.

The power of these systems is that the data held in any one cell on the 'paper' can be made dependent on that held in other cells, so changing a value in one cell can set off a chain reaction of changes through other related cells. This means that a model can be built in which the effect of changing key parameters may be observed (so called 'what if?' or sensitivity analysis).

1.2 BENEFITS OF SPREADSHEETS

Advantages of spreadsheets include:

- Automatic recalculation of values whenever any number is changed.

- The ability to process large quantities of data.

- Spreadsheets have the ability to display data in many different ways .i.e. numeric, tabular, graphical, and pictorial.

The automatic recalculation of formula values means that spreadsheets are particularly useful for:

- **Planning**, when the planner wants to produce a series of revised plans with different figures each time.

- **Sensitivity analysis**, whereby a plan or forecast can be tested for risk, by altering some of the number values in the table and seeing how this affects the other figures. For example, a forecast of future profits growth can be tested by altering the assumed rate of annual sales growth. If the assumed rate of growth is entered in a spreadsheet cell, all that is needed to do the sensitivity analysis is to alter the number in that cell.

Since a spreadsheet is used to create tables of figures, its usefulness for accounting might be readily apparent. Spreadsheets are widely used to:

- prepare financial forecasts

- prepare budgets and other plans

- produce reports comparing actual results with the budget

- prepare cash flow forecasts

- prepare financial statements.

1.3 LIMITATIONS OF SPREADSHEETS

There are limitations and problems associated with the use of spreadsheets that need to be controlled. These include the following:

- Spreadsheets for a particular budgeting application will take time to develop. The benefit of the spreadsheet must be greater than the cost of developing and maintaining it.

- Data can be accidentally changed (or deleted) without the user being aware of this occurring.

- Errors in design, particularly in the use of formulae, can produce invalid output. Due to the complexity of the model, these design errors may be difficult to locate.

- A combination of errors of design, together with flawed data, may mean that decisions are made that are subsequently found out to be wrong and cost the firm money. This is known as "spreadsheet risk" and is a serious problem. For example, a "cut and paste error" cost TransAlta $24 million when it underbid on an electricity supply contract.

- Data used will be subject to a high degree of uncertainty. This may be forgotten and the data used to produce, what is considered to be, an "accurate" report.

- Security issues, such as the risk of unauthorised access (e.g. hacking) or a loss of data (e.g. due to fire or theft).

1.4 FACTORS AFFECTING SPREADSHEET DESIGN

Spreadsheets are typically organic during design .i.e. they grow by adding columns and rows.

Design of the spreadsheet is often dictated by the volume of information that needs to be entered or displayed. Your computer screen will only be able to display a certain number of cells which you can comfortably read, so spreadsheets can be broken up across several worksheets within one workbook, or across several workbooks.

For example, one workbook might have twelve similarly formatted worksheets – one for each month of the year. This might comprise the company's annual forecast by month.

To access further worksheets than the standard three that you might be given, click on the tab at the bottom of the page which looks like a blank sheet of paper with a flash on it. Alternatively press 'Shift' and 'F11'.

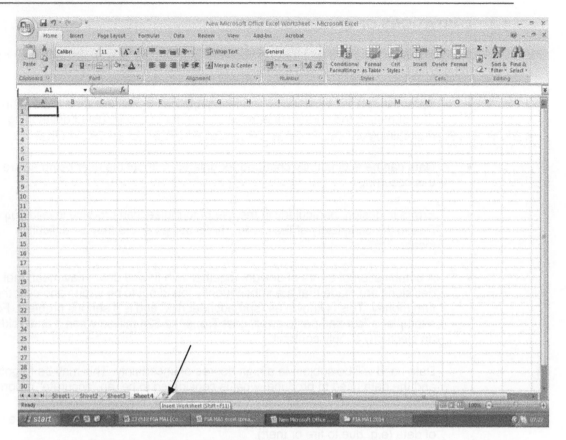

Features of a well-structured worksheet/workbook would include:

- It should be easy to use. Each worksheet, column and row should be labelled where applicable so that the user can navigate the spreadsheet quickly and with as few clicks as possible;

- It should be laid out in a user-friendly manner. It should be concise .i.e. not spread over too many unused cells, but not too squashed where the user finds it difficult to see, understand or insert data;

- The reader of the spreadsheet should be considered. Which is the most useful information for them? Perhaps this should be in a prominent place or could be highlighted.

ACTIVITY 1

What are the main advantages of using computers for a management information system? Are there any limitations to what computers can do to support management decision making?

For a suggested answer, see the 'Answers' section at the end of the book.

2 BASIC FEATURES OF A SPREADSHEET

For the purposes of describing spreadsheet features and functionality we have used the example of MS Excel. Similar features are found in all spreadsheet packages but the precise implementation methods will vary.

2.1 OPENING AND SAVING A SPREADSHEET

To begin work on a spreadsheet you will need to create one. You can do this by clicking on File, New, Microsoft Office Excel Worksheet. This will create a new file which can then be double clicked to open. A spreadsheet will appear which has three worksheets.

To save your spreadsheet, click on File, Save or Save As depending on where you would like to save your work.

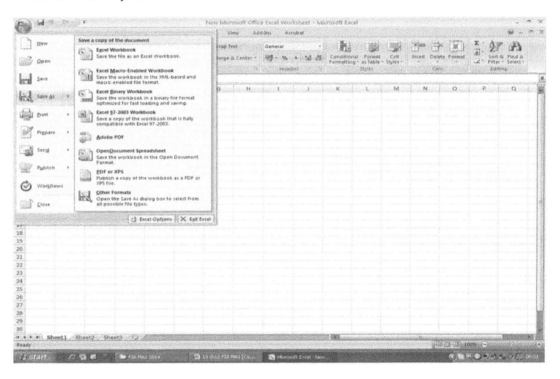

2.2 SPREADSHEET STRUCTURE

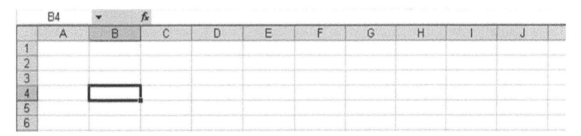

The spreadsheet [worksheet] shown above is made up of 'Rows', 'Columns' and 'Cells:

- The 'Rows' are numbered down the left hand-side from 1 – 65536

- The 'Columns' are lettered along the top from A – IV [256 columns]

- The 'Cells' are the junction of columns and rows [example cell A1 is the junction of Column A and Row 1]. There are 16,777,216 cells in a worksheet – far more than you will ever use.

- The 'Active' cell is where you are be able to enter data and is highlighted with a bold border [See B4 above]. Both the column letter and the row number are also highlighted

Note: Shortcuts

- Control+home takes you to cell A1

- Control+end takes you to the cell furthest into the worksheet that has been active [even if the content has been removed]

2.3 ACTIVATING SPREADSHEET FEATURES

There are many ways to activate many spreadsheet functions but two common ones are to use the toolbar at the top of the spreadsheet, or to right click on your mouse which shows a drop down menu of the most commonly used options.

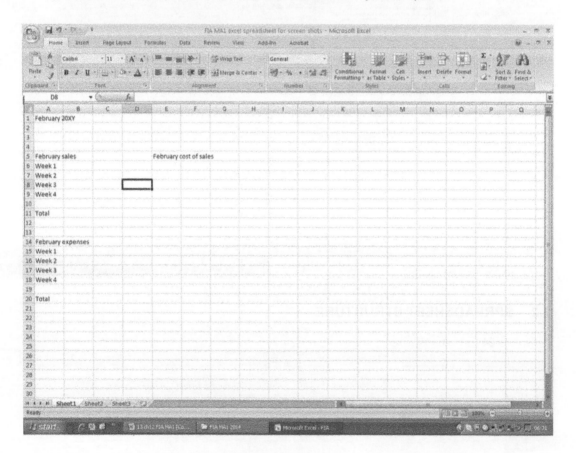

Or:

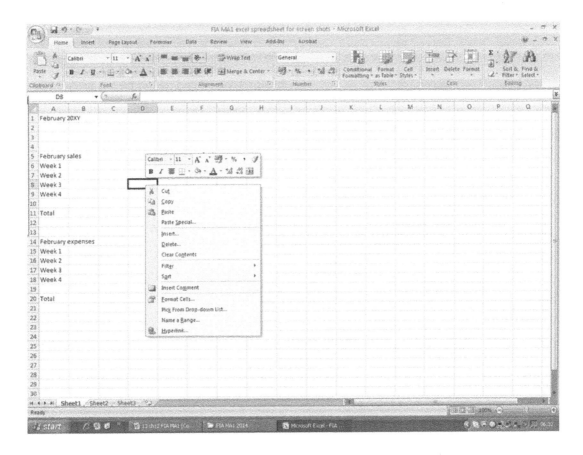

2.4 ENTERING DATA INTO YOUR WORKSHEET

Data can be entered into the 'Active Cell'. As this is done it will appear in the 'formula bar' and will stay there until you move away from the 'active cell'.

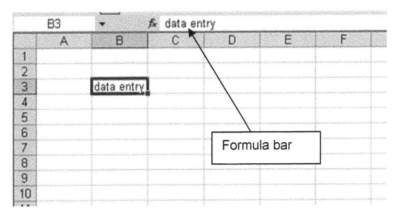

Data can also be entered into multiple cells. In the bottom right hand corner of the 'active cell' there is a little square block. If you hover over the block a 'cross' will appear. You can then 'click and hold' the left mouse button and then drag down, up, right or left to replicate the content of the 'active cell' in as many cells as you wish.

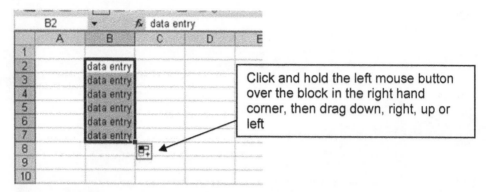

Note: Shortcuts

- Excel will try to guess if there is a sequence involved in your data entry. For example; weekdays, months, numerical sequences. If it can't find a sequence it will replicate exactly what you type into the 'Active Cell'.

- Excel will not guess a sequence for a single number. If you enter two numbers into adjacent cells, then highlight both cells, Excel will continue the sequence that you created.

2.5 COPY, PASTE AND PASTE SPECIAL

Excel allows you to copy data from the 'Active Cell[s]' to other cells. The simplest way to do this is as follows:

- 'Right-Click' the 'Active Cell[s]' and click 'Copy'.

- Go to the cell[s] you wish to copy to. 'Right-Click' and then click 'Paste'. What you have copied will appear.

There is another function 'Paste Special'. This function allows you to paste different aspects of what could be contained in a cell.

- 'Right-Click' the 'Active Cell[s]'. Click 'Copy'.

- Go to the cell[s] you wish to copy to. 'Right-Click and then click 'Paste Special'.

  Select what you want to happen from the menu that appears:

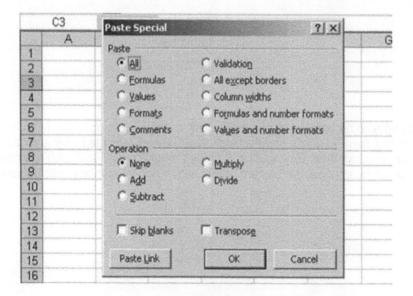

(i)   'All' pastes content, formula and formatting but it will not alter column width

(ii)   'Formulas' pastes the formula from the cell[s] to the new location. It maintains the structure of the formula but changes cell references accordingly – see example below. Note the formula in the formula bar. Do not worry about how formulas are written at this stage.

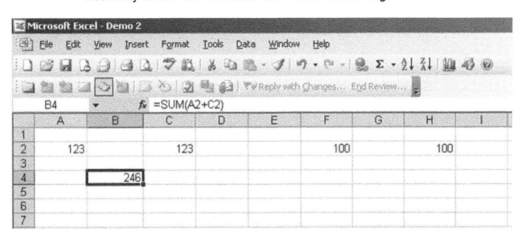

Now suppose the formula in cell 'B4' is copied to cell 'G4'. Excel works out that you want the formula to now refer to cells F2 and H2.

Note the formula in the formula bar:

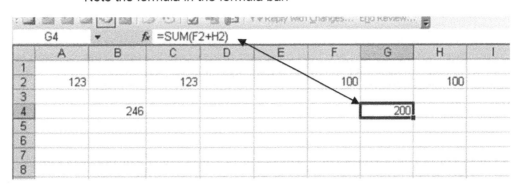

(iii)   'Values' pastes the value of a cell and not the formula that may have created the value

(iv)   'Formats' pastes any formatting that you might have carried out to the new cell[s]. This includes cell shading, borders and number formats, but not column width.

(v)   'Comments' pastes any comments that have been entered into a cell to the new location. 'Comments' allow you to write a note about a particular cell for you - and others - to see.

2.6 EDITING AND DELETING CELL CONTENT

There are a number of ways to edit cell content.

- Go to the 'Active Cell'. The content of the cell will appear in the formula bar. 'Left-Click' into the formula bar and you will then be able to edit the content. You can use the left and right arrow keys to move around.

- You can double 'Left-Click' into the active cell. You can then edit the content in the same way as above

To delete cell content you can do the following

- Go to the cell you wish to delete. Press the delete key. You can highlight multiple adjacent cells and delete in the same way.

- 'Right-Click' in the active cell and then 'Left-Click' clear cell contents. You can highlight multiple adjacent cells and delete in the same way.

- You can delete the content of non-adjacent cells by holding down the control key and 'Left-Clicking' the cells you wish to delete. Then press the delete key.

Note: If you 'Right-Click' a cell[s] and then click 'delete', Excel thinks you want to delete the cells completely. You will be offered a dialogue box asking you which way you want to shift the cells. This is a useful tool if it is your intention to shift data, but proceed with caution. You can always click 'Edit, Undo' or the undo icon on the toolbar if you change your mind.

2.7 SELECTING A RANGE OF CELLS

There are a number of ways to select a range of cells. One way of doing this is to highlight the first cell and then drag your mouse over the rest of the data you require. All cells (except the first one) you have selected will turn blue.

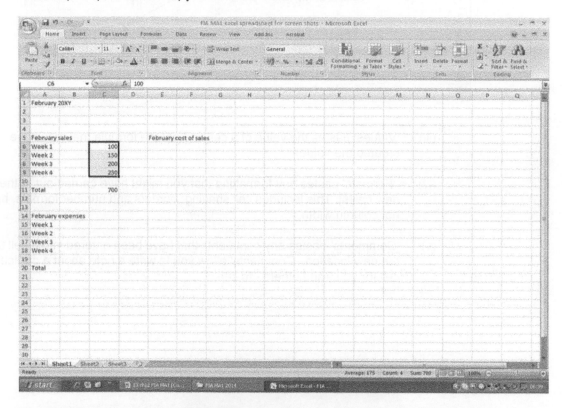

You can then right click for options of what to do with these cells .e.g. copy them to another part of your spreadsheet.

2.8 CAPTURING DATA FROM ANOTHER SOURCE

There is an option to import data from other sources, such as a word document or the internet. To access this press on 'Data' on the toolbar and on the left side there are five options in 'Get External Data'.

By clicking on 'From text', for example, this might take you to 'My Documents' where your Word files are kept or by clicking on 'From Web' it will allow you to enter internet addresses from which you may wish to insert data.

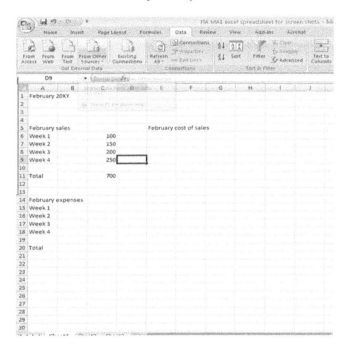

3 FORMATTING

Formatting is a process whereby you change the visual aspects of your worksheet. As a minimum it is useful if you can do the following:

1   Adjust row height and column width

2   Add borders and shading to cells and cell ranges

3   Format text and numbers

3.1 FORMATTING ROWS AND COLUMNS

Row height and column width can be changed to allow cell content to be visible. They can also be changed to allow a uniform size to rows and columns.

Starting with columns, the simplest approach is to do the following:

•   Highlight the columns you wish to change

•   'Right-Click'

•   'Column Width'

You will the following box appear and you can specify the width.

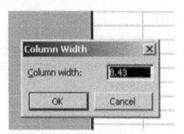

Exactly the same process can be followed to set row heights.

To insert or delete a row or column on your spreadsheet hover over the row number or column header and right click. A drop down menu will appear which will allow you to insert or delete.

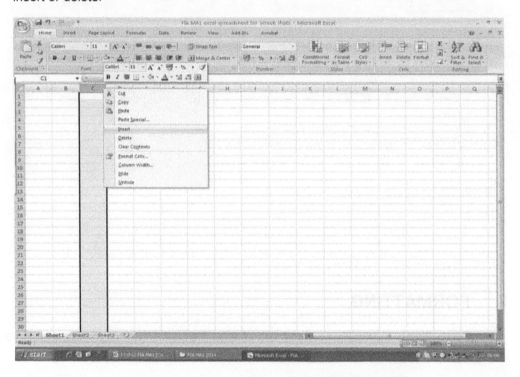

Alternatively you could go to the home tab and click on insert or delete:

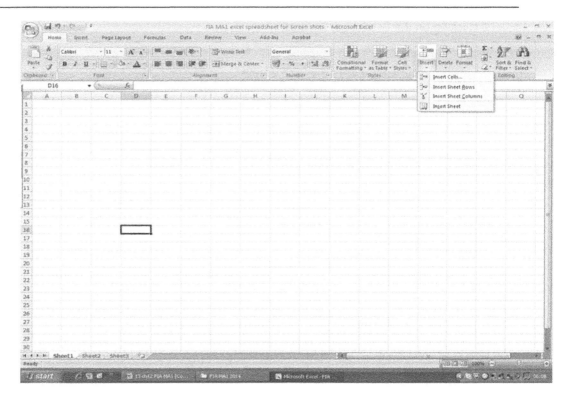

3.2 ADDING BORDERS AND SHADING

To adjust borders and shading, bring up the 'Format Cells' dialogue box by doing the following:

- Highlight the cells you wish to format.

- 'Right-Click' and then 'Format Cells

Below you can see the Format Cells dialogue box. Note the different tabs that can be selected. You will use this dialogue box a number of times in this chapter to format other parts of the worksheet.

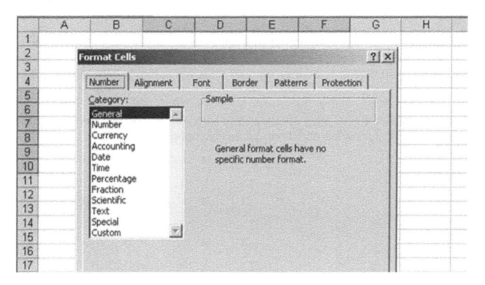

Clicking on the Border tab reveals:

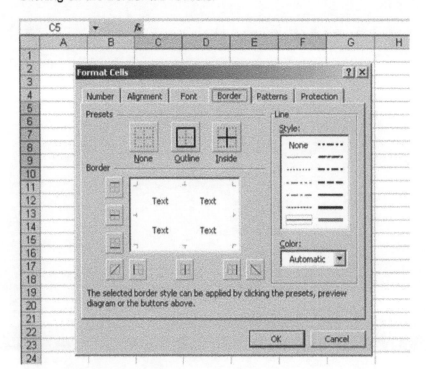

With the 'Border' tab opened you can now add borders to the cell or cells. You can create numerous types of border with different line thicknesses, styles and colour.

You can have different line thicknesses and colours in the same border if you wish. To create your border select your 'Style' and 'Colour' and then select the type of border you want.

It is common to add shading to cells to highlight them, especially when it comes to titles. We get to shading by following the path above and then clicking the 'Patterns' tab. Once there you can select either a colour for the cell[s] or a coloured pattern.

3.3 FORMATTING TEXT

Text entered into a cell will automatically 'align' to the left of a cell. 'Text' means any combination of letters and numbers. Numbers will automatically align to the right of a cell. Text or numbers entered into 'merged' cells will automatically align to the centre of the cells.

Excel will default to Arial, size 10, black and Regular. You do not have to accept the format that Excel provides and it can be easily changed.

Bring up the Format Cells dialogue box as before but this time click on the Font tab:

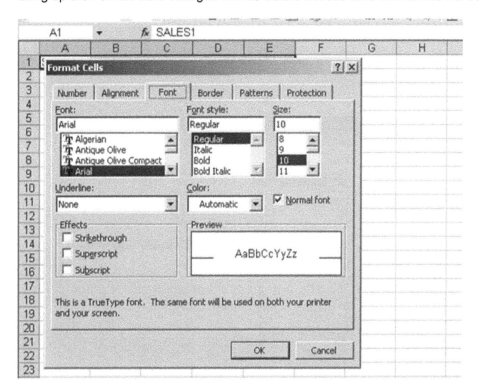

From the 'Font' tab you can choose a number of different effects. You can change the size, colour, style and also change the font itself.

From the 'Alignment' tab you can choose a number of different formats. You can choose to alter both the horizontal and vertical alignment of the text. You can change the direction of the text and you can also choose to have the text wrap itself within the cell, rather than go on continuously.

3.4 FORMATTING NUMBERS

You will want to format the numbers in your worksheet to give the reader the best chance of understanding what you are showing them.

Once again these are accessed from the Format Cells dialogue box, this time using the 'Number' tab:

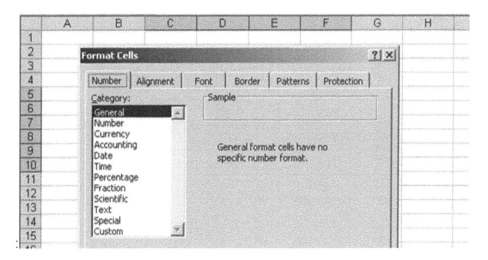

Number, Currency, Accounting and Percentage

Suppose you click on 'number'. The following options appear:

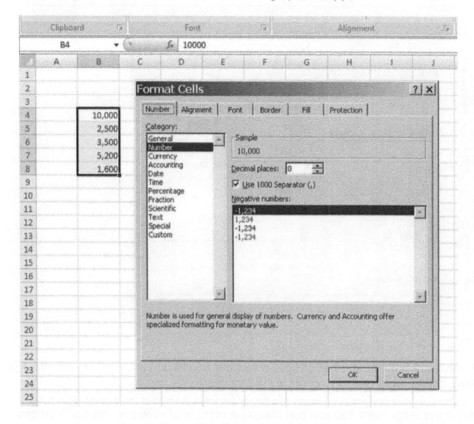

Here it is straightforward to specify the number of decimal places, whether or not you want a comma shown in larger numbers to indicate thousands and how to display negative numbers.

Note: If you format a cell to say '2' decimal places and then insert a number with '3' decimal places, Excel will round the number you enter to '2' decimal places. However, when you use the cell content to carry out a calculation you will find that Excel will use the full number [all 3 decimal places] and you could find that you don't get the answer you expect or that it appears not to 'cast' [add up].

Similarly, if you calculate numbers that result in more decimal places than you format for, Excel will use the number that is calculated.

Depending on which category you click on, you will be able to adjust the following characteristics:

	Decimal Places	Negative number format	1000 Separator	Currency symbol
Number	Yes	Yes	Yes	–
Currency	Yes	Yes	Auto	Yes
Accounting	Yes	–	Auto	Yes
Percentage	Yes	–	–	–

Date and time formats

Date formats are serial numbers that represent the number of days since January 1st 1900. This is how spreadsheets can calculate the number of days lapsed between 2 dates.

Date formats can be accessed from the numbers tab. If you click on 'Date' you will be presented with numerous date formats and also a location. Selecting a particular date format does not mean that dates need to be entered in this way. A number of different ways of writing dates can be entered and Excel will format it to your selection. You must, though, enter the year if you want any year other than the current year. If a spreadsheet doesn't understand the date format it will enter it as text.

Time Formatting

Time formats are also serial numbers. Here the serial number represents a fraction of a day. The day is based on the non-day of January 0 1900. To get the correct time format you must put a colon between the hours and minutes, and the minutes and seconds for the spreadsheet to recognise what you are trying to do.

Date with Time Formatting

You can add a time to a date by first entering the date followed by a space and then the time in the 00:00 format. The time will only show in the formula bar, however, Excel will add the time as a fraction of the day and use it in any subsequent calculation.

Custom formats

In the custom number drop down list there are a number of formats that can be changed by the user to a format of their own. Alternatively you can create your own number format and save it here.

For example, it is here that you can create a number format that allows you to have negative numbers in red with brackets representing the negative symbol. The format below would give numbers that have no decimal places and negative numbers would be shown in Red with a minus sign

#,##0;[Red]-#,##0,   Result would be **-1,234**

You can change this to get rid of the minus sign and replace it with brackets

#,##0;[Red](#,##0),   Result would be **(1,234)**

4   FORMULAE

Once you have populated your spreadsheet with data you will need to use formulae to create information that can be used.

4.1   OPERATORS AND THE ORDER OF PRECEDENCE

You are going to use simple mathematical functions to analyse your data but in order that you can do this you need to understand the order in which Excel calculates.

Excel uses operators [each of which has a symbol] in these mathematical functions.

Below is a list of the order of precedence.

Operator	Symbol	Order of Precedence
Exponentiation (powers)	^	1
Multiplication	*	2
Division	/	2
Addition	+	3
Subtraction	-	3

4.2 PARENTHESES (BRACKETS)

The order of precedence determines which operators Excel will use 1st in its calculations. It can be seen above that Excel will 1st calculate multiplication or division before it does addition.

Not only can you override this by using parentheses it is extremely important that you are able to do so in order that your calculations provide the correct answer [the one you intended]. By inserting Brackets around part of a formula it forces Excel to calculate the content of the brackets 1st, followed by the remainder of the formula. You can have multiple sets of brackets in a formula as you will see in later sessions when you deal with more complex situations.

4.3 SIMPLE FORMULAS

Any and all formulas that you input must start with an equals sign [=] otherwise Excel will not know what you are doing and treat your entry as text.

To highlight the need for putting brackets around numbers let us assume that you want to add together B4 and C4 and then multiply this result by a 3rd number D4, giving the answer in cell F4. If you highlight cell F4 and type in

= B4+C4*D4

Then the spreadsheet will show the following

	A	B	C	D	E	F	
1							
2							
3							
4		4	3	5		=B4+C4*D4	

If you then press Enter, cell F4 will now show the result of the calculation. The formula can still be seen in the formula bar when the cell is active.

Without brackets Excel will give a total of 19, which unfortunately is not what you wanted. Excel has done the multiplication first rather than the addition. However, with brackets enclosing (B4+C4) you will get the result you require which is 35.

	A	B	C	D	E	F	
1							
2							
3							
4		4	3	5		=(B4+C4)*D4	

Note: Instead of typing in the cell references, you could have clicked on the relevant cell at the appropriate stage in the formula:

- Type: =(

- Click on cell B4

- Type: +

- Click on cell C4

- Type:)*

- Click on cell D4

- Press 'enter'

4.4 SUM AND AVERAGE FUNCTIONS

Sum

Suppose you want to add up a column of figures, say B4 down to B8 inclusive and show the answer in cell B9.

	A	B	C	D	E	F	G
1							
2							
3							
4		10,000					
5		2,500					
6		3,500					
7		5,200					
8		1,600					
9							
10							

It would be relatively straightforward to enter the formula in cell B9

> = B4 + B5 +B6 +B7 +B8

However, there are a number of ways to do this more quickly in Excel.

The easiest is to recognize that Excel has many standard functions already set up. One way to see this is to click on the formula bar while cell B9 is active and type

> = S

The following options will appear, each of which is a standard function.

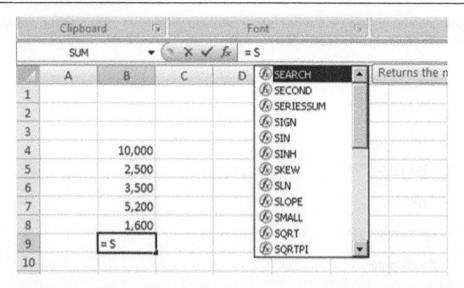

If you scroll down you will find the SUM function, which you can then double click.

Excel now wants you to enter which cells you want summed.

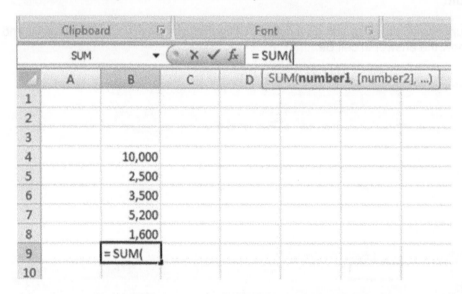

There are (at least) three ways to complete the entry of the formula:

- Type in B4:B8) and press 'enter', or

- Click on cell B4, type the colon, click on cell B8, type the closing bracket and press 'enter', or

- Click on cell B4 and hold the mouse button down. Then drag the cursor to cell B8 and press 'enter'.

Average

Exactly the same process can be done for the averaging function:

* = AVERAGE (B4:B8)

* Type: = A to get the list of functions starting with A

Note: the information that goes inside the brackets of a function is known as the 'argument'.

Auto-sum functions

Auto-Sum is a time-saving tool that Excel provides. It has quite useful functionality but it does not give you all the flexibility that creating your own formulas would. Auto-Sum is represented by the Greek letter Sigma (Σ) and is the mathematical summation symbol. It can be found on the standard toolbar at the top of the screen.

There are 5 options with auto-sum including Sum and Average.

4.5 ROUND FUNCTION

The Round function returns a number rounded to a specified number of digits.

The syntax for the Round function is:

Round(number, digits)

number is the number to round. Alternatively a cell reference can be used.

digits is the number of digits to round the number to. If the digit is set to 1 it will round to 1 decimal place, 2 will round to 2 decimal places. If the digit is set to -1 it will round to the nearest 10, -2 will round to the nearest 100 etc.

Consider the following:

	A	B	C	D	E
1	164.44				
2					
3					

A formula in cell B1 of = round(A1,0) would return a value of 164. If the formula was =round(A1,-1) it would return a value of 160.

4.6 IF FUNCTION

The IF function is used when we want a cell to display one of two results depending on a previous set of data. It is a very useful formula which can be used to perform calculations, display text or combine both.

The syntax for the formula is as follows:

=IF(logical_test,value_if_true,value_if_false)

This can be put into simpler language as follows:

=IF("if the condition stated here is true", "then enter this value", "otherwise enter this value")

Let's look at an example. Consider the following data for a business that has an agreement to give a £50 discount to a major customer on every invoice.

	A	B	C	D
1	Invoice Value (pre-discount)	Discount	Invoiced total	
2	$	$	$	
3	224	50	174	
4	497	50	447	
5	865	50	815	
6	28	50	0	
7	1,066	50	1,016	
8				

The business can't have a negative invoice total and this is why cell C6 needs to display a nil balance. In order to achieve this, the following IF function would be used:

= IF(A6-B6<0,0,A6-B6)

What this tells the spreadsheet to do is: check whether A6 minus B6 is less than zero, if the answer is yes then display a zero, otherwise display the answer for A6 minus B6.

The IF function is very versatile and it can be used to provide text solutions as well as numbers as results. It is therefore a very popular spreadsheet function.

5 ERRORS IN FORMULAE

Despite our best efforts mistakes occur when setting up formulae. Fortunately Excel has a number of ways of highlighting and helping to resolve errors. Here we show the most common problems found.

5.1 FORMULA AUTOCORRECT

When writing formulas sometimes parentheses [Brackets] get left out or placed in the wrong order, or you might enter the wrong number of arguments [syntax error].

Formula AutoCorrect will pop up on screen and offer to correct the problem. Whilst Excel is very good at finding errors you do need to be careful as it sometimes guesses incorrectly.

For example, suppose you type in one too many brackets into a SUM formula as follows:

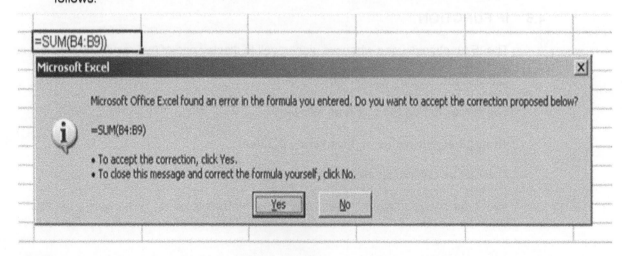

In the example above Excel has correctly determined that one too many parentheses have been placed in the formula. In this instance you can accept the offered solution.

5.2   DIVIDING BY ZERO ERRORS

You cannot divide a number by zero as that would give an infinite result. If you mistakenly do this, then excel will show the following alert:

In the above example Excel has put a flag in the cell where it thinks there is an error. If you click into the error cell you will be given the option to review and deal with the error.

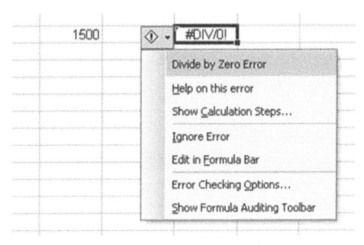

Above you can see a Divide by zero error. You now have the opportunity to get help from a number of sources, or ignore the error.

- If you click 'Help on this error' the Excel Help system will pop up and you can ask questions and seek help from here

- You can choose to ignore the error. This is OK if you know what the problem is and can fix it, but you should not simply ignore the error as you will create problems elsewhere.

- Edit in formula bar puts the cursor in the formula bar, and you can fix your problem

- 'Show calculation steps', 'Error checking options' and 'Show Formula Auditing Toolbar' are beyond our scope here.

5.3 CIRCULAR REFERENCES

A circular reference is a common error and occurs when you try to include the cell that we are writing a formula in as part of the formula.

For example:

If you typed the following formula into Cell **A3**, you would get a circular reference message.

$$=SUM(A1+A2+A3)$$

The circular error is because to determine the value of A3 via the SUM, then you already need to know the value of A3 as part of the argument. Excel would show the following:

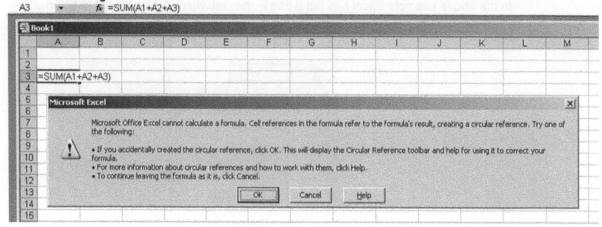

- OK or Help will present the Help facility

- Cancel, leaves the error in the formula. You should only do this if you want the circular reference. It is possible to want to do this, but, it is beyond this syllabus, therefore, don't do it.

5.4 TYPES OF ERROR

We have considered two type of error. Here is a more complete set:

Error	Description
#DIV/0!	This occurs where we have tried to divide by zero or a blank cell.
#NAME?	This occurs when we use a name that Excel doesn't recognise. This is common in incorrectly spelled function names
#NUM!	This occurs when you place an invalid argument in a function
#REF!	This occurs when a formula uses an invalid cell reference
#VALUE!	This occurs when we attempt to use an incorrect data type

6 OTHER USEFUL SPREADSHEET FUNCTIONS

Spreadsheets can not only perform calculations but they can also be used to summarize and analyse data. The following are some of the useful functions that help in doing this.

6.1 THE SORT FUNCTION

The sort can be used to sort data into a particular order in order to make the data easier to understand for users. There are various ways that a user might want to do this such as:

- Alphabetically. A user may want to re-arrange a list and put it in alphabetical order. The list can also be sorted by reverse alphabetical so that data appears with the last alphabetical reference appears first.

- Numerically. Data can be sorted numerically. Again there are two ways to do this – from highest to lowest or from lowest to highest.

Performing the function is straightforward. A user simply highlights all the data that they want to sort, chooses the sort function (either from the menu or from a specialized icon on the toolbar), and then determines which sort to apply and which columns to apply it to.

Consider the following unsorted data:

	A	B	C	D
1	Name	Amount		
2		$		
3	John	100		
4	Helen	200		
5	Adnan	400		
6	Jamil	50		
7	Barus	100		
8				

The key when sorting data will be to highlight all the data – in this example both the name and the amount. Let's assume that the user wants to sort this data from highest amount to lowest amount and then alphabetically. It doesn't matter if the user includes the titles as these will not be sorted. So the user could highlight all the data from A1 to B7 then choose the sort function.

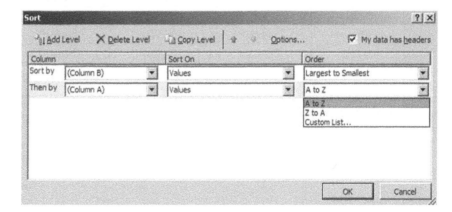

In the sort function the user would select to sort by column B first and choose largest to smallest, then sort by column A next and choose to sort by A to Z. The output would then be:

	A	B	C	D
1	Name	Amount		
2		$		
3	Adnan	400		
4	Helen	200		
5	Barus	100		
6	John	100		
7	Jamil	50		
8				

So that when there are two amounts for $100, Barus comes first alphabetically.

6.2 THE FILTER FUNCTION

Filtering is used to temporarily 'hide' data that the user does not want to see. Filtered data displays only the rows that meet criteria that the user specifies. The function can be found from the spreadsheet menu or some programmes such as Microsoft Excel have a specialist icon on the toolbar (in Excel the filter function looks like a funnel).

Filters are commonly found in database spreadsheets that hold a large amount of data. It may well be that the user doesn't want to see all of this data and only wants to examine a sub-set of the entire data. For example, a database might contain data on the salaries of all staff. But perhaps the user only wants to see director salaries. A filter could be used to temporarily hide the salaries for all non-directors and only display salaries paid to directors.

You can also filter by more than one column. Filters are additive, which means that each additional filter is based on the current filter and further reduces the subset of data viewed.

Consider the following data (this is a small extract from a company's overall salary database):

	A	B	C	D
1	Name	Role	Department	Salary (£)
2				
3	John	Salesman	Sales	15,000
4	Peter	Director	Sales	44,000
5	Mikel	Accountant	Finance	23,000
6	Zhu	Director	R&D	36,000
7	Sayed	Director	Sales	14,000
8				

Let's say we want to only see directors who work in the sales department. The steps involved in achieving this are:

1   Highlight the data (cells A1 to D7)

2   Click on the Filter option

3   An arrow ▼ will appear alongside each heading

4   On column B click on the arrow that has appeared and it will bring up a list of data that we can choose to hide. Hide Accountant and Salesman by un-ticking those boxes.

5   On column C click on the arrow and un-tick all departments except Sales.

The spreadsheet should now look like this:

	A	B	C	D
1	Name ▾	Role ▾	Department ▾	Salary (£) ▾
2				
4	Peter	Director	Sales	44,000
7	Sayed	Director	Sales	14,000
8				

You can see that only the data that we want to see now appears. The remaining data is temporarily hidden (though it has not been deleted. It can be retrieved by removing the filters by reversing the process above. Columns which have had a filtered applied have a slightly different icon (which in excel looks like ▾.)

This can be a useful tool that ensures that users only get the information that they need and that one spreadsheet can satisfy the needs of many different users. For example, a different user could use the same spreadsheet but apply different filters so that only the salaries for everyone in the sales department are shown.

6.3   ADDING COMMENTS TO A CELL

Sometimes you may want to add comments to data on your spreadsheet but the comment may take up space which makes the spreadsheet layout less attractive. Comments can be added which are 'hidden' until your cursor hovers over them.

To do this, go to the cell which you would like to comment on, right click and in the drop down menu there will be an 'Insert comment' option.

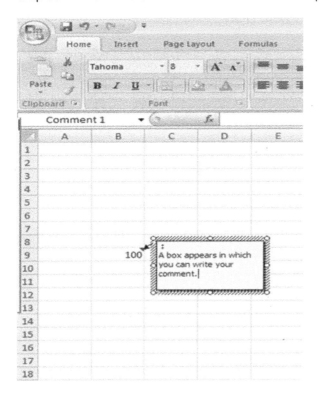

The reader can see that there is a comment underlying the data by the red marker at the top right of the cell.

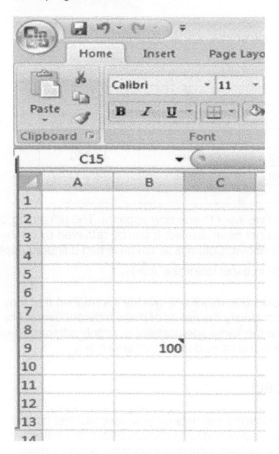

To delete any comments, go to the relevant cell and right click. The drop down menu will give you the option to 'Delete comment'.

6.4 THE FIND AND REPLACE FUNCTION

Sometimes you may want to use data from an existing spreadsheet but change a small amount of that data. For example, you may have produced a budget for January using a spreadsheet. The budget may be similar for February. If you copy the January spreadsheet to another worksheet called February, the only change required might be to identify every 'January' and change it to 'February'. This would be much faster than creating the spreadsheet from scratch.

To do this there is a Find and Replace function:

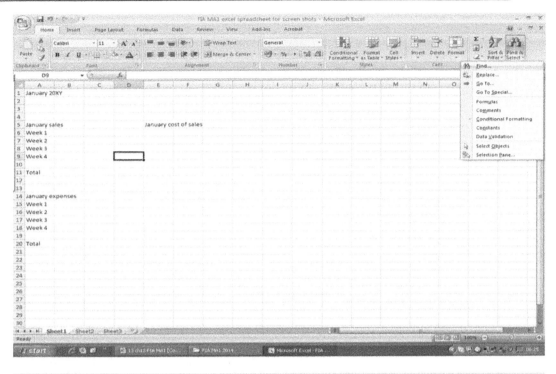

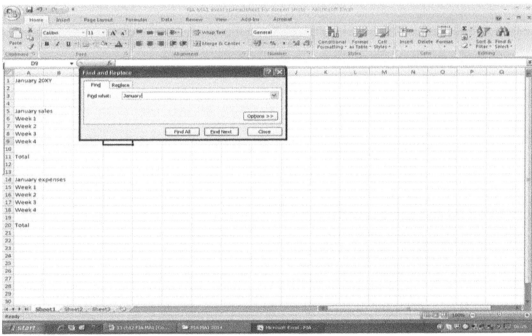

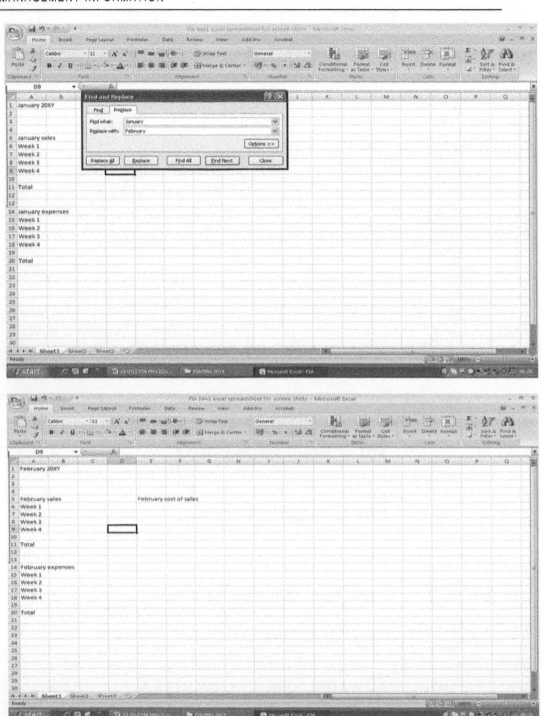

7   PRESENTING INFORMATION – CHARTS AND GRAPHS

A major advantage of spreadsheets is how easy it has become to produce impressive looking charts and diagrams.

Within spreadsheets there are two basic ways to display charts and graphs. There is no right or wrong way - it is user preference. It is also a simple matter to switch between the two types.

- **Chart Sheet**, here the chart or graph becomes the entire worksheet.

- **Embedded**, here the chart or graph is located on the sheet that contains the data. The chart can be moved around to suit the user.

7.1   BAR AND COLUMN CHARTS

Suppose the sales of companies A and B are as follows:

	Company A	Company B
UK	59.3	60.2
EU, outside UK	61.6	69.0
Europe, outside EU	10.3	11.1
North America	15.8	18.0
Australasia	9.9	8.8

To show this data in a diagram of some sort, highlight all the cells above and click the following:

- 'Insert' tab

- Click on the bottom RH corner of the 'chart' tab to reveal all the different types of chart

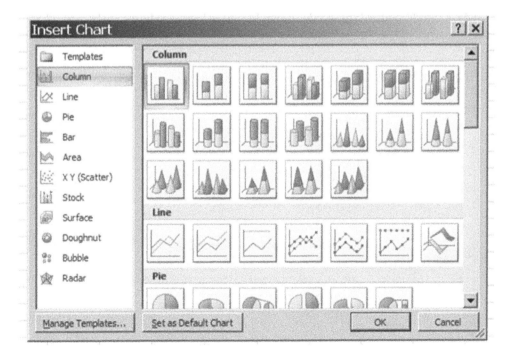

For example, clicking on the first option would give:

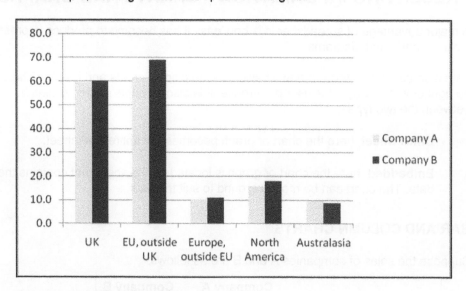

Clicking on the top right icon would give:

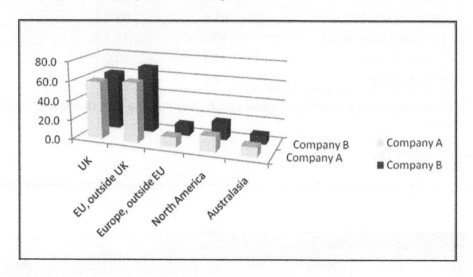

The second option on the second row would give

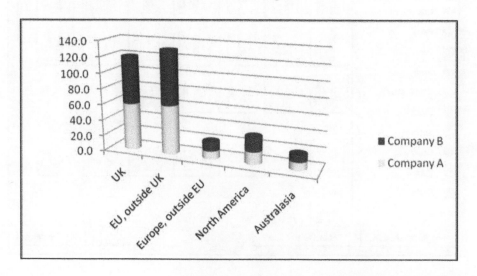

All of these demonstrate a number of things, for example,

- that Company B has achieved higher sales in all regions except Australasia

- that the EU, outside the UK is the region with the highest sales

- and that sales are virtually the same in the UK

Note: You can change the colours by clicking on the relevant part of the legend and then clicking on the format tab.

Advantages

- Bar charts are particularly good for making comparisons, such as those between products, regions and companies, as seen above.

- Trends can also be easily identified – for example, if each column represented a different period

Disadvantages

- Can give a misleading impression, depending on how the axes are labelled – especially if a key variable, such as sales, does not start at zero

- It can become confusing if there are too many components.

- Small components can be difficult to assess and add little value to the chart.

Suitability: Bar charts are particularly good for making comparisons

7.2 LINE CHARTS

Line charts are particularly good for showing trends.

For example, suppose the sales for 5 years of two products, X and Y, were as follows

	Product X	Product Y
2005	510	450
2006	530	480
2007	600	560
2008	650	640
2009	570	660
2010	590	720

Highlighting these cells in a spreadsheet and accessing the 'Insert chart' box gives the following (and other) graphing options:

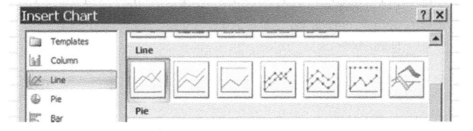

Clicking the first option gives the following:

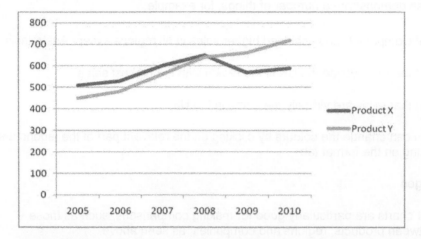

From this chart it is easy to see, for example, how Product X has seen higher growth and was less affected by the economic downturn in 2008/9.

Advantages

- They are good at showing specific values of data, meaning that given one variable the other can easily be determined.

- They show trends in data clearly, meaning that they visibly show how one variable is affected by the other as it increases or decreases.

- They enable the viewer to make predictions about the results of data not yet recorded

Disadvantages

- Can give a misleading impression, depending on how the axes are labelled – for example, if vertical and horizontal axes have different scales or one does not start at zero

- It can become confusing if there are too many lines.

- Difficult to compare graphs with different scales

Suitability: Line charts are particularly good for showing trends

7.3 PIE CHARTS

Pie charts can be accessed using the same 'Insert chart' box. For example, the sales of Company A above can give the following pie charts.

	Company A
UK	59.3
EU, outside UK	61.6
Europe, outside EU	10.3
North America	15.8
Australasia	9.9

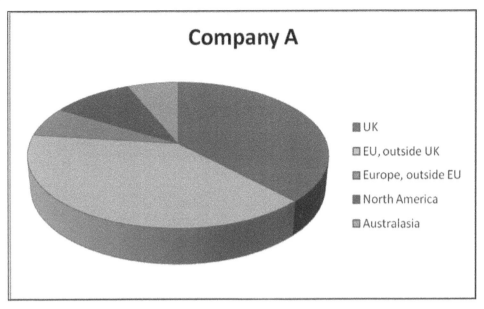

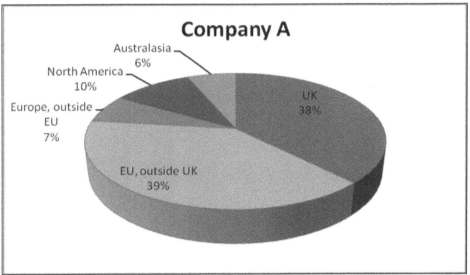

Advantages

- Quick and easy to identify the largest and smallest proportions relative to the total – for example it is easier to see that sales in EU, outside the UK were the greatest for Company A.

- Good at showing proportional or relative significance

- Immune to distortion due to changes in scale.

Disadvantages

- Gets harder to read and process as the number of slices or segments increases

- Exact values and totals are not immediately obvious.

- Can be difficult to discern relative slice proportions when they are similar in size unless additional data is added to the chart (see the second variation above).

- Difficult to compare different pie charts

- Difficult to show change over time.

Suitability: The pie chart is a simple information graphic whose principal purpose is to show the relationship of a part to the whole.

7.4 SCATTER DIAGRAMS

Scatter diagrams are very useful when trying to see if a relationship ('correlation') exists between two sets of data.

For example, suppose we are looking at how advertising influences sales and have the following data:

Advertising	Sales
150	3050
170	3260
185	3270
200	3600

Highlighting the data and using the first option from the 'X-Y scatter' charts gives the following:

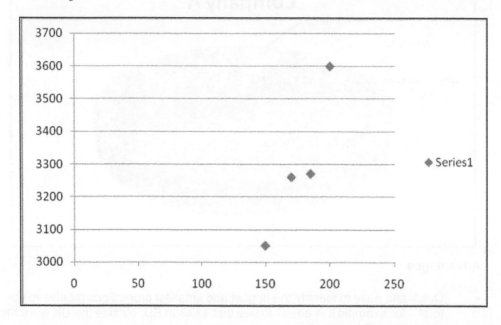

While the chart is highlighted, click on 'layout' and 'trendline' allows you to put a trend line linking the data:

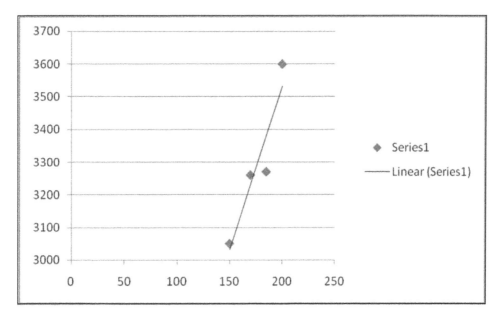

Advantages

- Help determine if two attributes are correlated

- Need many data points to be reliable

Disadvantages

- Hard to interpret with lots of observations (the more measurements, the more dots)

- People may see relationships that don't exist

Suitability: scatter diagrams are very useful when trying to see if a relationship ('correlation') exists between two sets of data.

7.5 AREA CHART

An area chart displays a series as a set of points connected- by a line, with all the area filled in below the line. It is an extension of a line graph. It is used to show overall totals (the top line) as well as the components from different sources (the different shades).

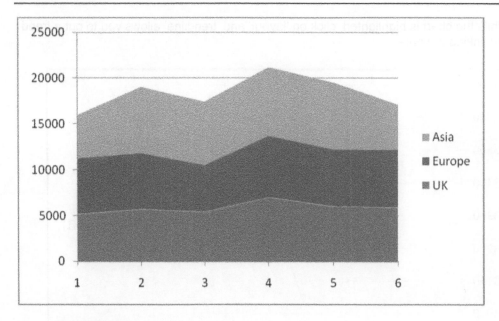

Advantages

* Both the overall total and the component elements can be illustrated.

* Trends in components and in the total can be easily identified.

* The graph illustrated uses an absolute scale to prepare the chart (i.e. the absolute total is used). A percentage scale can be used instead where the total must always come to 100% and this can be more useful in identifying the relative size of each component against each other.

Disadvantages

* Only one overall total can be displayed.

* It can be difficult to assess the relative size of each component as the absolute data is difficult to determine. For example, would a user be able to judge the amount of European sales in quarter 3 just from looking at the graph? They would be able to identify that the sales have fallen but it would be very difficult to put a definite value on the size of the fall.

* It can become confusing if there are too many components.

* Small components can be difficult to assess and add little value to the chart.

Suitability: Area charts are best used to display over time how a set of data adds up to a whole (cumulated totals) and which part of the whole each element represents.

7.6 MULTIPLE GRAPH TYPES ON ONE CHART

Also known as Combination Charts these charts must consist of at least two data series. With this chart type you can have either two graph types on one axis or insert a second value or 'Y' axis.

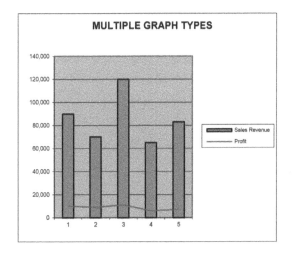

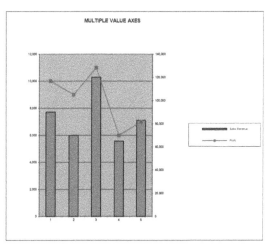

These graphs combine the advantages of the two graph types used. But they can become more confusing for users and require further explanation.

8 HOW TO CREATE CHARTS IN SPREADSHEETS

In order to create a graph or chart in a spreadsheet the user must go through four stages:

1   Select the data

2   Open the chart wizard

3   Choose the chart type

4   Choose chart options

Each of these stages will now be examined in turn.

Note: Every spreadsheet package will have its own particular processes for creating charts in spreadsheets but they will all follow the same basic principles and structure. In this section we will use Microsoft's Excel spreadsheet programme to illustrate each stage but other packages will give similar displays and results.

8.1 SELECTING THE DATA

Graphs and charts can be created from almost any set of data, but it is often best if it is first assembled into a table in order to separate data into its constituent parts (say, sales (possibly split by product) and time).

To select the data you want to use you simply highlight the relevant table or part of the table. If the data is not adjacent to each other you will have to select more than one section of the table. To do this you should highlight the first section required, press and hold the control key on your keyboard, and then select the second section. If more sections are needed you repeat this process until all relevant areas of the table (or tables) are highlighted.

Consider the following table which shows a company's sales over a number of years:

	A	B	C	D	E
1		20X0	20X1	20X2	20X3
2	**Product A**	40	45	48	51
3	**Product B**	80	82	78	66
4	**Product C**	22	30	41	54
5					
6	**Total**	142	157	167	171
7					

Let's assume we wanted to make a column chart which shows sales split by component for each year. We would select all the cells from A1 to E4. We would exclude the 'Total' row (A6 to E6) as we do not want to show that on our chart, and we should always ignore blank rows (A5 to E5).

8.2 OPENING THE GRAPH WIZARD

To add a graph in Microsoft excel we need to click on the insert tab and a view of possible graph types will be displayed. (This applies to Microsoft Excel 2007. For older versions, we would need to click on insert, then chart wizard, then choose our chart type to achieve the same result.

8.3 CHOOSE THE CHART TYPE

We now need to select our chart type. There are icons for the most popular types of chart, but we can access other chart types by clicking on the drop down menu. Let's click on the 'column chart' icon, and a 2D version (3D versions simply add more volume to the graph and is used if we want the graph to have a more visual effect).

This will convert the table and display a column chart as follows:

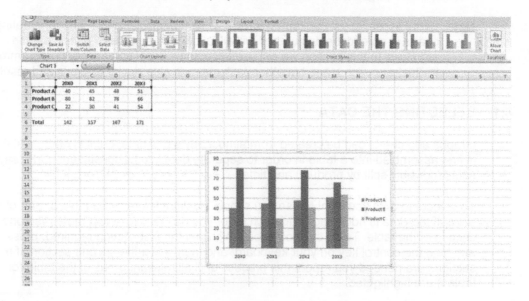

From the tabs at the top of the spreadsheet we can do many things now with our chart:

- *Change chart style* will allow us to convert the chart to a pie chart, line graph etc.

- *Select data* will allow us to change the data we are using to create the chart

- *Chart styles* will allow us to change colours, graphics etc.

- *Move chart* will allow us to move the chart to a new or already created sheet within the document. To move the chart around the existing sheet we simply drag and drop it.

8.4 CHOOSE CHART OPTIONS

Clicking on the layout tab at the top of the spreadsheet will bring up for areas such as:

- *Chart Titles* and *Axis Titles.* Charts should have suitable titles and often the axes on bar or line graphs will need titles. The program will try and use any row or column headings if you include them when selecting data but the results may not be appropriate every time and this is where you can change them.

- *Legend.* This is the small box or set of boxes, initially located to the right of the chart if switched on. It provides a key to the different columns, for example, in the columnar chart. If there is only a single box then it is pretty useless and should be switched off. Legends are only relevant when you have a chart which compares similar data for two or more groups on the same chart. The bars will be in different shades or colours, one shade or colour for each group. A legend will show which is which.

- *Data labels.* These would put selected information on the chart, close to the appropriate element of the chart. They could be names for pie chart segments or numbers on columns or a line at certain points. Useful for pie charts but they often clutter up other displays.

- *Data table.* This facility can be used to add the table of selected data to the chart window. Useful if you haven't published the figures elsewhere and the information is not obvious from the chart alone.

- *Axes.* You will not need to change this often. Sometimes not displaying one of the axis lines can make the chart clearer but you would probably need to use labels or other identifying features in those cases to ensure the chart remains relevant and not just a 'picture'

- *Gridlines.* These are the horizontal lines at various steps up the y-axis on bar and line graphs. In this option you can choose whether or not to display them.

In the following example, a chart title has been chosen added to the chart, horizontal gridlines have been turned off and the legend has been moved below the chart:

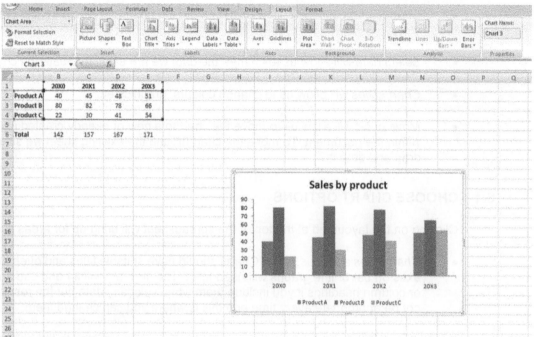

The completed chart can then be transferred to other sheets within the spreadsheet or even to other documents (such as reports created in Microsoft Word), where end-users can consider and analyse them.

9 CONSOLIDATING INFORMATION

9.1 MULTIPLE WORKSHEETS

Spreadsheets have the ability to work with and on more than one 'worksheet' at a time. Most spreadsheets start with three blank worksheets to which the user can add more if they wish. A user can easily move between worksheets and can even link data together from different worksheets. Working with multiple worksheets is no different to working with multiple documents or ledgers by hand. For example, each separate spreadsheet might record the sales or expenses for different departments or divisions.

It is useful to give each worksheet its unique, identifying name to improve navigation for users. This name can be used in calculations that rely on different information contained in different spreadsheets.

For example, an accountant has four worksheets in one spreadsheet with the following names:

- UK Division

- Asian Division

- African Division

- Total

Each of the first three worksheets shows a breakdown of sales for each division by product and has an overall sales total in cell J90. Let's say in cell J90 on the total division we wanted to total the sales from each division. The following formula would be used:

= +'UK Division'!J90+'Asian Division'!J90+'African Division'!J90

Note how the name of each division is in inverted commas and has an exclamation mark at the end. Other than that, this is similar to the simple addition formula used earlier in the chapter. It also means that if a change is made in one individual worksheet it will be updated on the total spreadsheet

9.2 CONSOLIDATING DATA

An alternative method to simply adding together information from different worksheets is to consolidate the worksheets into one overall master worksheet (which can be named as the 'Total' worksheet if the user desires). This is an easier way to work when the data in each worksheet is in the same layout and has the same column and row headings.

Consolidation is accessible from the data menu. When a user clicks consolidation they simply have to highlight the areas that they want to consolidate one at a time and 'add' them to the list of data to be consolidated. The function will then add the totals together from each individual worksheet into one overall total worksheet.

The limitation with this method is that if changes are subsequently made in an individual worksheet the consolidated worksheet will not be updated. The consolidation process will have to be repeated.

10 SPREADSHEET SECURITY

In some spreadsheets it may be useful to add an element of security to the spreadsheet by restricting access or the content that can be viewed etc. There are various reasons for doing this such as protecting against accidental or malicious changes, protecting copyright or intellectual property, or ensuring that only certain users can access a spreadsheet.

It is important when designing a spreadsheet that these security issues are considered before the spreadsheet is issued to users.

There are various ways to achieve this:

10.1 HIDING ROWS OR COLUMNS

Rows or columns can be hidden from view so that a user cannot see them. This is often done to hide formulae or workings which might confuse an untrained user.

To hide a column or row you first need to select the column or row by clicking on the letter at the top of the column or the number to the left of the row to select it. You can select more than one column or row at the same time by highlighting several of the row or column labels together.

To hide the range selected you right click on the mouse and a format menu appears as below. To hide the range you need to select the **Hide** option.

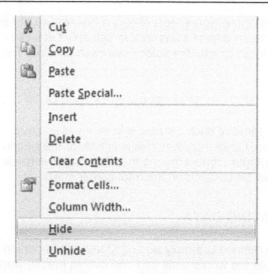

You will no longer be able to see the hidden data but you will know that there is some hidden data because the column letter or row number will no longer be displayed. For example, in the following spreadsheet, we know that column C has been hidden because if we read the letters for the column headings we can see that it skips from column B to D.

	A	B	D	E
1	**VAT Rate**	20%		
2		Net	Gross	
3			$	
4	Sale 1	600	720	
5	Sale 2	500	600	
6	Sale 3	300	360	
7	Sale 4	400	480	
8				

If you want to unhide a row or column then you need to select the rows or columns to either side of the hidden data. For example, in the above table we would select columns B and D. A right mouse click will bring up the format menu again, where the final option is Unhide. Clicking this will make the hidden column reappear.

10.2 PASSWORD PROTECTING A SPREADSHEET

It is possible to limit access to an entire spreadsheet by adding password protection so that only users who know the password can access the spreadsheet.

To access this option you need to go through the 'Save as' procedure (this should be familiar from section 2.1). Before clicking on the 'Save' option you will notice in the bottom left hand corner of the pop-up menu a 'Tools' drop menu:

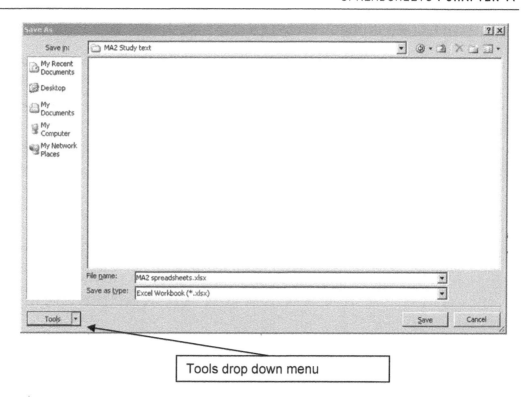

Tools drop down menu

Clicking on 'Tools' will pop up menu, from which you need to select General Options, which in turn will pop up the following:

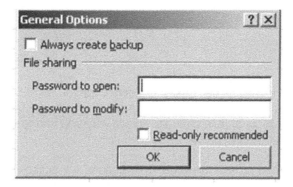

You can now apply one or two passwords. The 'Password to open' option will mean that any user who wants to open the spreadsheet must have the relevant password. You can also allow users to open the spreadsheet but restrict their ability to make changes to it. To do this you need to add a password in the 'Password to modify' box. The user will be able to read the spreadsheet but will not be able to make any changes unless the correct password is input.

The biggest issue with the use of passwords is ensuring that they are known and remembered. If a password is lost there is no way to recover the password or to undo the security measures that have been added.

If you select the 'Read-only recommended' option, the user will be prompted to open the file as read-only unless changes will be made. You can use this option without requiring a password. This is a safety net that makes users think twice before making changes to the document, but they can choose to ignore this warning if they want. It is therefore less secure than requiring a password.

10.3 PROTECTING INDIVIDUAL CELLS

You can protect individual cells if you choose (such as those containing a formula) whilst allowing users to change other cells. For example, you might have a formula in a cell that calculates the VAT on a net invoice once a user inputs the net amount. So you would want the user to be able to change the net amount but not be able to change the way in which the VAT is calculated. To do his involves two stages:

Firstly select the cell (or cells) that you **do not** want to protect. You then need to bring up the 'Format Cells' dialogue box (as explained earlier in the chapter) and choose the 'Protection' tab.

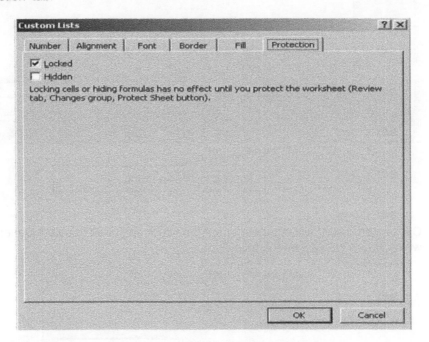

To protect an individual cell then the 'Locked' option must be ticked. This is automatic in most spreadsheets, and therefore you must un-tick the box for the cells that you want the user to be able to change. This is why you had to start by selecting the cells that you do not want to protect.

Next you have to protect the sheet. Instructions are actually given in the diagram above. Alternatively you can right click on the sheet name (at the bottom of the spreadsheet and the option will appear in a pop-up menu:

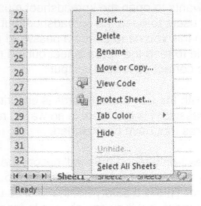

When you choose the 'Protect Sheet' option a final pop-up appears:

You can then choose what a user can do, such as change the formatting, edit data, delete rows or columns etc. As a final measure of security you can choose to add a password that must be entered before anyone can undo this process.

To undo the cell protection the second stage can be repeated, where the option will now have changed from 'Protect Sheet' to 'Unprotect Sheet'.

11 PRINTING

When a spreadsheet is complete and has been reviewed a user is likely to want to print it to paper.

If you want to print only part of your spreadsheet you should highlight it by left clicking and dragging the mouse over the relevant area. Once selected, you should click the office button at the top of the screen to access the drop down menu which allows you to 'Print'. Clicking on print brings up a box that asks you to 'Print what' and you can choose to print your 'selection'.

There are dedicated 'quick print' icons in most spreadsheets which will print the entire spreadsheet. The problem with this approach is that it will print out everything from cell A1 to the final cell that has data in it. This could be cell EE5000 and cover hundreds of A4 pages!

It is therefore important to only print what is needed and to print it to the size and format that is required. Therefore, before printing a spreadsheet a user should enter the page setup menu to configure the spreadsheet for printing.

Firstly access the 'Print Preview' function from the spreadsheet menu.

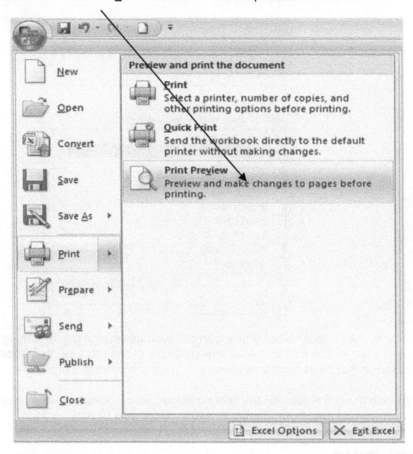

This allows the user to see how the print out currently looks. Before clicking on the 'Print' icon the user should click on 'Page Setup' to ensure the page is properly set up before final printing.

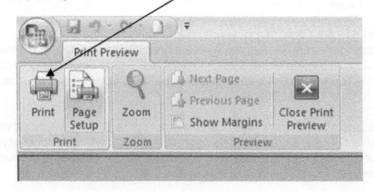

This will allow for the following options:

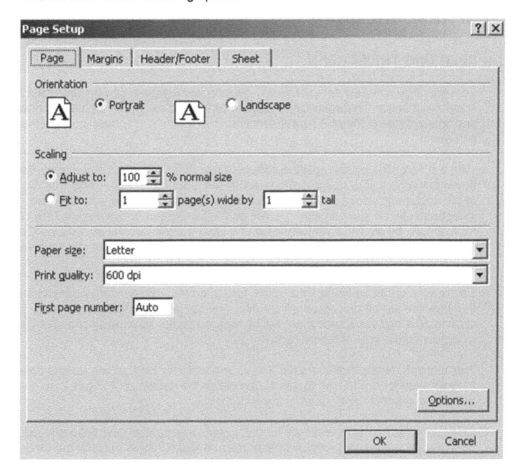

- **Page setup**

    In this area the user can choose the size of print and the type of paper to be used in the printer. The user can even condense the entire worksheet to one page if they choose.

- **Margins setup**

    In this area the user chooses how much blank border should surround the spreadsheet on a page.

- **Header/footer settings**

    In this section a reader can add headers and footers to act as titles for each print out. A user can also add page numbers if they choose to do so.

- **Sheet setup**

    In this area the user can choose which part/area of the spreadsheet to print and whether to print the gridlines that normally appear in spreadsheets to separate cells. The user can also choose to repeat certain rows at the top of each page if the spreadsheet runs to more than one page.

12 FURTHER ASPECTS OF WORKING WITH SPREADSHEETS

12.1 SPLITTING THE SCREEN

For very large spreadsheets there may be more to view than can be seen on a single computer monitor. There are many ways in which you can view more of the document and one of these is the split screen function. The function is accessible from the 'view' sub-menu.

With this function you can split the screen at any point by having a horizontal line anywhere across your document in order to split your document in two. The two part of the document, above and below the line will then be viewable and workable independently. So you can input figures on the top screen above the line (this could, for example, be showing the beginning of a cash budget calculation) and watch the results on the bottom part of the screen below the line (which might for example be displaying the overall net cash inflow or outflow for the month).

Each element can be worked on, scroll, formatted etc. independently despite the fact that they are still on one spreadsheet. The line can be removed at any time by double clicking on it and the spreadsheet will be merged again, keeping all changes you have made during the split of the screen.

This function means that users don't have to constantly be scrolling up and down a long spreadsheets and also that they can watch the impact of changes from one part of the document on other parts of the document.

Splits can also be made vertically for documents that spread over too many columns. Or, if needed, users can employ both horizontal and vertically splits at the same time to allow work on and viewing of four parts of a spreadsheet at once!

12.2 FREEZE PANES

Another problem with large spreadsheets is that as the user moves around they can lose the titles that are necessary for referencing. The user can easily lose track of what data is contained in the columns and rows forcing them to scroll all the way to top or all the way to the left just to see what data they are looking at. In order to 'freeze' the titles in place the freeze panes function is used.

The freeze panes function is accessible from the view menu. Once a cell has been selected the freeze panes function will freeze the columns to the left and the rows above that selection. When the user scrolls around the spreadsheet these frozen rows and columns will remain in view, allowing the user to continue to get heading references etc. This means that no matter how far down the spreadsheet that the user scrolls, the rows above the freeze pane will always be viewable. Likewise, no matter how far the user scrolls to the right, the columns to the left of the freeze pane will always be viewable.

Note: the chosen freeze point can be any cell, anywhere on the spreadsheet, though if headings start on row 1 then usually a user will select cell A1. The spreadsheet will then freeze the titles on the first row and first column.

CONCLUSION

Spreadsheets are very useful and flexible business tools. They can perform many varied types of calculation and can be used to represent information in a variety of forms.

Spreadsheet functions can be used to increase the efficiency of many accounting tasks. However it is important that the spreadsheet is secure against unwanted access and changes.

Spreadsheets can be used to link various types of information together and to print out this information in a manner that is most useful to the user.

KEY TERMS

Spreadsheet – a computer program that allows numbers to be entered and manipulated.

Bar chart – a diagram to represent data where the height of the 'bar' represents a value.

Pie chart – a diagram to represent data where the area of a circle is used to represent a value.

Scatter graph – a diagram used to illustrate the relationship between two sets of numbers.

Area chart – a diagram where the area under a line represents a value.

SELF TEST QUESTIONS

		Paragraph
1	Give three advantages of spreadsheets	1.2
2	What is 'spreadsheet risk'	1.3
3	Name six different ways to format a number	3.4
4	How would you correct a #DIV/0! Error?	5.2
5	Explain how to consolidate data	7.2

EXAM-STYLE QUESTIONS

1 Which of the following types of diagrams would be best used to show the relationship between two sets of numbers?

 A Bar chart

 B Pie chart

 C Area chart

 D Line graph

2 Which of the following symbols represents the multiplication symbol on spreadsheets?

 A +

 B ^

 C *

 D /

3 The use of which of the following functions is most likely to only show the user the data that they want to see?

 A Sort

 B Filter

 C Split screen

 D Freeze panes

4 An accountant wishes to use a spreadsheet to calculate budgeted production.

Which formula should go in cell C5?

	A	B	C	D
1		**Jan**	**Feb**	**March**
2		Units	Units	Units
3	Sales (units)	1000	1200	1250
4	Opening inventory finished goods	100	110	120
5	Production (units)		?	

 A =C3-D4+C4

 B =C3-C4

 C =C3+D4

 D =C3+D4-C4

5   An accountant wishes to use a spreadsheet to calculate the production volume ratio for a period.

	A	B	C	D
1		**Budget**	**Actual**	
2	Production (units)	1,000	1,200	
3	Hours worked	200	250	
4	Rate per hour	$15	$15.20	
5				

Which formula would correctly calculate the production volume ratio?

A   =C2*B3/B2

B   =C2/B2

C   =B2/B3*C2

D   =C3/B3

For the answers to these questions, see the 'Answers' section at the end of the book.

KAPLAN PUBLISHING

ANSWERS TO CHAPTER ACTIVITIES AND EXAM-STYLE QUESTIONS

CHAPTER 1

ACTIVITY 1

A purchasing department would have the responsibility for purchasing all goods and materials, keeping suppliers' records, researching new sources of supplies and negotiating terms and discounts. Types of staff would include buyers and order assistants.

ACTIVITY 2

Advantages

1   In order to prepare a procedures manual it is necessary to examine the systems and procedures carefully. The close attention paid to the systems and procedures can only benefit the organisation, in that strengths and weaknesses are revealed.

2   Supervision is easier.

3   It facilitates the induction and training of new staff.

4   It assists the organisation in pinpointing areas of responsibility.

5   Having been written down in the first place, systems and procedures are easier to adapt and/or change in response to changing circumstances.

Disadvantages

1   There is an associated expense in preparing and maintaining the manuals not least in terms of staff time.

2   To be of continuing use the manuals must be updated regularly.

3   The instructions may be interpreted strictly and implemented too rigidly.

EXAM-STYLE QUESTIONS

1 **D** Giving better service to department management is one of the advantages of decentralisation.

2 **D** The transport clerk will generally report to the marketing manager. The Finance Manager will be responsible for all the financial affairs of the organisation and may have the following staff:

Financial accountant

Cost accountant

Management accountant

Chief cashier

Clerks positions for wages, costing, ledgers and credit control.

3 **B** Books of prime entry are the books in which all transactions are initially recorded.

In a business there will be a large number of transactions each day, making it very difficult to record individual transactions directly to the general ledger. That is why we usually group similar transactions together, and record them in one of the books of prime entry. Periodically, the totals of each group of transactions are transferred to the general ledger.

4 **B** In an integrated system all of the accounts are maintained in one ledger and there is no need for a cost ledger control account. Answer A would be the entries in an interlocking system, where financial accounts such as cash, debtors and creditors are not maintained in the cost ledger. Answer C is incorrect because the expense was incurred for credit, not paid for in cash. Answer D uses the correct accounts but the entries are the wrong way round.

CHAPTER 2

EXAM-STYLE QUESTIONS

1 **A** Cost accounting can be used for inventory valuation to meet the requirements of both internal reporting and external financial reporting.

2 **C** Management information must be cost effective, sufficiently accurate and consistent. It is often impossible to provide information immediately as some processing and analysis of data must be carried out.

3 **C** Personnel records would be collected for a variety of purposes and therefore would be secondary data. All of the other data are collected specifically for the task and so are primary data.

CHAPTER 3

ACTIVITY 1

		Direct costs		Indirect costs	
Cake production		*Tablecloth production*			
Choc chips	$150	300m cotton cloth	$2,500	Rent of building	$1,000
Cake decorator's time	$60	Sewing machine operators	$800	Electricity bill	$220
Cardboard cake boxes	$40				
Total	$250		$3,300		$1,220

EXAM-STYLE QUESTIONS

1   **C**   This is a simple definition of a fixed cost. Option B is incorrect because the fixed cost per unit falls as the level of output increases.

2   **C**   Straight-line depreciation is a fixed cost. All of the other costs vary with the volume of production.

3   **c**   An indirect cost is a cost that cannot be traced directly to a specific cost unit.

CHAPTER 4

ACTIVITY 1

EDSP

ACTIVITY 2

(i)   110/124/204

(ii)   110/123/203

(iii)   111/120/205

(iv)   111/126/205

(v)   110/103/210

(vi)   110/125/204

EXAM-STYLE QUESTIONS

1   **B**   300 for York followed by 500 for travel costs followed by 630 for the sales function.

2   **B**   Mnemonic means something that aids the memory or understanding. This uses an alphabetical coding rather than a numerical coding system. It is often used to abbreviate or simplify information.

3   **C**   Overhead costs should be coded to a suitable overhead cost centre.

CHAPTER 5

ACTIVITY 2

FIFO results in later purchases remaining in inventory. The calculations are as follows.

FIFO

	Units	$	
Opening inventory	50	350	(50 units at $7)
1 Feb: Purchases	60	480	
	110	830	(50 at $7, 60 at $8)
1 March: Sales	(40)	(280)	(40 at $7)
	70	550	(10 at $7, 60 at $8)
1 April: Purchases	70	630	
	140	1,180	(10 at $7, 60 at $8, 70 at $9)
1 May: Sales	(60)	(470)	(10 at $7, 50 at $8)
Closing inventory	80	710	(10 at $8, 70 at $9)

		Sales $	Cost $	Profit
Profit on sale	1 Mar	400	280	120
	1 May	720	470	250
	Total			370

LIFO

	Units	$	
Opening inventory	50	350	(50 units at $7)
1 Feb: Purchases	60	480	
	110	830	(50 at $7, 60 at $8)
1 March: Sales	(40)	(320)	(40 at $8)
	70	510	(50 at $7, 20 at $8)
1 April: Purchases	70	630	
	140	1,140	(50 at $7, 20 at $8, 70 at $9)
1 May: Sale	(60)	(540)	(60 at $9)
Closing inventory	80	600	(50 at $7, 20 at $8, 10 at $9)

		Sales $	Cost $	Profit
Profit on sale	1 Mar	400	320	80
	1 May	720	540	180
	Total			260

AVCO

	Units	$	Weighted average
Opening inventory	50	350	$7
1 Feb: Purchases	60	480	
	110	830	($830/110) = 7.5455
1 March: Sales	(40)	(302)	(40 at $7.5455)
	70	528	(50 at $7.5455)
1 April: Purchases	70	630	
	140	1,158	($1,158/140) = $8.2714
1 May: Sale	(60)	(496)	(60 at $8.2714)
Closing inventory	80	662	(80 at $8.2714)

		Sales $	Cost $	Profit $
Profit on sale	1 Mar	400	302	98
	1 May	720	496	224
	Total			322

Periodic weighted average pricing

The periodic weighted average price = $\dfrac{350 + 480 + 630}{50 + 60 + 70}$ = $8.11

The value of issues is 100 × $8.11 = $811

The closing inventory value is:

	Units	$
Opening inventory	50	350
1 Feb	60	480
1 April	70	630
	180	1,460
1 March	(40)	(324)
1 May	(60)	(487)
Closing inventory	80	649

		Sales ($)	Cost ($)	Profit
Profit on sale	1 Mar	400	324	76
	1 May	720	487	233
				309

EXAM-STYLE QUESTIONS

1   **B**   A material requisition note is a document used internally for requisitioning a quantity of inventory from the stores.

2   **D**   Glue would normally be classified as an indirect cost as it would be uneconomical to allocate the amount of glue used for each toy directly.

3   **B**   The store's manager would normally authorise a purchase requisition when inventory is low and pass this to the purchasing department to raise a purchase order.

4   **A**   LIFO = 400 × $3.40 + 525 × $3.00 = $2,935

5   **C**   AVCO = $3.20 × 275 + $3.00 × 600 + $3.40 × 400 = $4,040

         $4,040/1,275 = $3.17 per unit × 925 = $2,932

6   **D**   FIFO = 275 × $3.20 + 600 × $3.00 + 50 × $3.40 = $2,850

CHAPTER 6

ACTIVITY 1

	$
Basic pay (40 hours × $10)	400.00
Overtime hours (5 hours × ($10 × 1.5))	75.00
	———
Weekly wage cost	475.00
	———

Alternatively this could be shown as:

	$
Basic pay (45 hours × $10)	450.00
Overtime premium (5 hours × ($10 × 0.5))	25.00
	———
Weekly wage cost	475.00
	———

The overtime payment for the week is $75 and the overtime premium is $25.

The overtime premium is the additional amount over the basic rate of pay that is paid for the overtime hours rather than the total payment made for the overtime hours.

ACTIVITY 2

80 units × $3 = $240

ACTIVITY 3

Total weekly wage

	$
Monday (12 × $6)	72
Tuesday (14 × $6)	84
Wednesday (guarantee)	50
Thursday (14 × $6)	84
Friday (10 × $6)	60
	——
	350
	——

The payment of a guaranteed amount is not a bonus for good work but simply an additional payment required if the amount of production is below a certain level.

ACTIVITY 4

The amount the employee will be paid will depend upon the exact wording of the agreement. Production of 102 units has taken the employee out of the lowest band (up to 99 units) and into the middle band (100 – 119 units). The question now is whether **all** his units are paid for at the middle rate ($1.50), or only the units produced in excess of 99. The two possibilities are as follows:

(a)   102 × $1.50 = $153.00

(b)   (99 × $1.25) + (3 × $1.50) = $128.25

Most organisations' agreements would apply method (b).

ACTIVITY 5

Total bonus	$20,000
Split between 50 employees ($20,000/50) =	$400 per employee
Managing director's bonus	$400
Chris Roberts' bonus	$400

ACTIVITY 6

Managing director's bonus

$$($48,000 × 0.016) = $768$$

Chris Roberts' bonus

$$($18,000 × 0.016) = $288$$

ACTIVITY 7

Time saved 30 minutes.

At a wage rate of $10.00 per hour the labour cost saving is $5.00.

This employee's efficiency has saved the organisation $5.00. The basis of a bonus scheme for time rate workers is that a proportion of this $5.00 should be paid to the employee as a bonus. The manner in which the proportion is calculated must now be considered.

ACTIVITY 8

		$
Basic rate	$\dfrac{36}{60}$ × $12	7.20
Bonus	$\dfrac{60-36}{2}$ × $\dfrac{\$12}{60}$	2.40
		———
Total payment for job A		9.60
		———

ACTIVITY 9

			$
Basic rate	$\dfrac{36}{60} \times \$12$		7.20
Bonus	$\dfrac{36}{60} \times (60 - 36) \times$	$\dfrac{\$12}{60}$	2.88
Total payment for job A			10.08

ACTIVITY 10

(a) Actual production for the week   120,000 units

Standard production for the week

480 hours × 200 units   96,000 units

Excess production   24,000 units

Bonus percentage	$=$	$\dfrac{24,000}{96,000} \times 50\%$
	$=$	12.5%
Bonus rate	$=$	12.5% × $10
	$=$	$1.25 per hour

The total bonus to split between the group is therefore:

480 hours × $1.25   = $600

(b) Total pay for Jones

	$
Basic pay 42 hours × $8.00	336.00
Bonus 42 hours × $1.25	52.50
	388.50

ACTIVITY 11

(a) Labour cost per unit for 45 units is $2 per unit.

(b) Labour cost per unit for 80 units is $\dfrac{(50 \times \$2) + (25 \times \$2.20) + (5 \times \$2.40)}{80}$

$= \dfrac{\$167}{80} = \$2.09$

EXAM-STYLE QUESTIONS

1　**B**

			$
James:	Basic rate of pay	$6.20 per hour	
	Overtime rate of pay	$6.20 × 1½ = $9.30 per hour	
	Overtime rate of pay (weekend hours)	$6.20 × 2 = $12.40 per hour	
	Basic pay	40 hours at $6.20	248.00
	Overtime pay	5 hours at $9.30 per hour	46.50
		3 hours at $12.40 per hour	37.20
			_____
	Total		331.70
Jake:	Basic rate of pay	$7.40 per hour	
	Overtime rate of pay (first 6 hours)	$7.40 × 1½ = $11.10 per hour	
	Overtime rate of pay (excess hours)	$7.40 × 2 = $14.80 per hour	
	Basic pay	35 hours at $7.40	259.00
	Overtime pay	6 hours at $11.10 per hour	66.60
		7 hours at $14.80 per hour	103.60
			_____
	Total		429.20

2　**D**　The overtime premium is the amount over and above the hourly rate paid for overtime hours. In this case 3 hours at $4 (½ × $8) per hour = $12.

3　**C**　The idle time and overtime premium will be indirect costs and the remaining costs will be direct costs. The total wages are the hours worked at the basic rate plus the overtime premium 40 × $8 + $12 = $332. Of these the idle time (6 × $8) and the overtime premium of $12 will be indirect = $60

4　**C**

49 units at $2.25 = $110.25

30 units at $2.50 = $75.00

7 units at $2.75 = $19.25

Total of $204.50

5　**C**

The employee works 37 × 60 minutes = 2,220 minutes.

In this time it is expected that 2,220/48 = 46.25 products are produced.

54 products have been produced, which is 54 − 46.25 = 7.75 more than expected.

This represents a total cost saving of 7.75 × 48/60 × $6.80 = $42.16

The employees' total wages are therefore 37 × $6.80 + 42.16/2 = $272.68

6   **C**

The employees' gross pay is their net salary plus deductions made.

$2,500 + $250 + $375 = $3,125

CHAPTER 7

ACTIVITY 1

$$\text{Overhead absorption rate} = \frac{\$40,000}{80,000 \text{ units}}$$

$$= \$0.50 \text{ per unit}$$

ACTIVITY 2

$$\text{Overhead absorption rate} = \frac{\$20,000}{80,000 \text{ hours}}$$

$$= \$0.25 \text{ per hour}$$

Overhead to be included in cost of product J:

2 hours × $0.25   = $0.50

ACTIVITY 3

		Job no. 958
		$
	Direct materials	270.00
	Direct labour	126.00
	Direct expense – machine hire	150.00
(a)	**Prime cost**	546.00
	Production overhead (14 hours × $3)	42.00
(b)	**Total production cost**	588.00
	General overheads (10%)	58.80
(c)	**Total cost**	646.80

EXAM-STYLE QUESTIONS

1   **A**   The rule says that if something is purchased for use in the business over a long period of time (a machine, factory or car), then the expenditure will be classified as a fixed asset. Fixed asset expenditure is classified as capital expenditure.

On the other hand, expenditure incurred on 'everyday items' (for example repairing a machine or a car) or the 'running costs' is generally classified as revenue expenditure.

2   **B**   Overhead absorption rates are predetermined and are therefore based on the budgeted figures.

Overhead absorption rate   = $128,000/25,000

= $5.12 per direct labour hour

3   **A**

Overhead absorption rate   = $96,000/25,000 = $3.84 per direct labour hour

Overhead absorbed   = $3.84 × 26,000 actual hours

= $99,840

Overhead incurred $108,000

_____

Under-absorption $8,160

_____

The overhead is under absorbed because less overhead was absorbed than was actually incurred.

4   **B**

	$
Actual expenditure	56,389
Absorbed cost (12,400 × 1.02 × $4.25)	53,754
	———
Total under-absorption	2,635

5   **D**

Fixed production overheads are over-absorbed when actual expenditure is less than budget and/or actual production volume is higher than budget.

CHAPTER 8

ACTIVITY 1

Absorption costing

	Year 1 $	Year 2 $	Year 3 $	Year 4 $	Total $
Sales	1,000	1,500	2,000	3,000	7,500
Opening inventory @ $7.60	–	1,520	2,280	2,280	6,080
Variable costs of production @ $4	1,200	1,000	800	800	3,800
Fixed costs @ $\frac{900}{250}$ = $3.60	1,080	900	720	720	3,420
	2,280	3,420	3,800	3,800	13,300
Closing inventory ($4 + $3.60) $7.60	1,520	2,280	2,280	1,520	7,600
Cost of sales	(760)	(1,140)	(1,520)	(2,280)	(5,700)
(Under)/over-absorption (W)	180	Nil	(180)	(180)	(180)
Net profit	420	360	300	540	1,620

Working

Calculation of over/under-absorption

Fixed cost control account

	$		$
Incurred:		Absorbed:	
Year 1	900	300 × $3.60	1,080
Over-absorption	180		
	1,080		1,080
Year 2	900	250 × $3.60	900
	900		900
Year 3	900	200 × $3.60	720
		Under-absorption	180
	900		900
Year 4	900	200 × $3.60	720
		Under-absorption	180
	900		900

Marginal costing

Item	1st year	2nd year	3rd year	4th year	Total
	$	$	$	$	$
Sales	1,000	1,500	2,000	3,000	7,500
Variable cost of sales (@ $4)	400	600	800	1,200	3,000
Contribution	600	900	1,200	1,800	4,500
Fixed costs	900	900	900	900	3,600
Net profit/(loss)	(300)	–	300	900	900

EXAM-STYLE QUESTIONS

1   B

In absorption costing inventory is valued at full production cost, which includes variable production overhead and absorbed fixed production overhead.

2   B

Fixed production overhead per unit = $48,000/12,000 units = $4.

Sales volume is less than production volume by 280 units.

In absorption costing, this means that some fixed overheads will be carried forward in the closing inventory value. Fixed overheads in this addition to inventory = 280 units × $4 = $1,120.

In marginal costing, all fixed overheads incurred in a period are charged as an expense against profit. Marginal costing profit would therefore be lower than the absorption costing profit by $1,120.

3   C

There was an increase in inventory in the period; therefore the absorption costing profit is higher than the marginal costing profit (because a larger amount of fixed overhead is carried forward in the closing inventory value).

	$
Marginal costing profit	72,300
Less: fixed costs in opening inventory (300 units × $5)	(1,500)
Add: fixed costs in closing inventory (750 units × $5)	3,750
Absorption costing profit	74,550

4   A

Profit figures only differ if inventory changes in the period.

CHAPTER 9

ACTIVITY 1

JOB COST CARD

Job number: 3867   Customer name: OT Ltd

Estimate ref: Quoted estimate:

Start date: 1 June   Delivery date: 17 June

Invoice number: Invoice amount:

COSTS:

Materials

Date	Code	Qty	Price	$
1 June	T73	40 kg	$60	2,400
5 June	R80	60 kg	$5	300
9 June	B45	280m	$8	2,240
				4,940

Labour

Date	Grade	Hours	Rate	$
1 June	II	43	5.80	249.40
2 June	II	12	5.80	69.60
	IV	15	7.50	112.50
5 June	I	25	4.70	117.50
	IV	13	7.50	97.50
9 June	I	15	4.70	70.50
				717.00

Expenses

Date	Code	Description	$

Production overheads

Hours	OAR	$

ACTIVITY 2

As the machinery is used in equal proportions on three different jobs then only one third of the hire charge is to be charged to Job 3867 ($1,200 × $\frac{1}{3}$ = $400).

JOB COST CARD

Job number: 3867   Customer name: OT Ltd

Estimate ref: Quoted estimate:

Start date: 1 June   Delivery date: 17 June

Invoice number: Invoice amount:

COSTS:

Materials

Date	Code	Qty	Price	$
1 June	T73	40 kg	$60	2,400
5 June	R80	60 kg	$5	300
9 June	B45	280m	$8	2,240
				4,940

Labour

Date	Grade	Hours	Rate	$
1 June	II	43	5.80	249.40
2 June	II	12	5.80	69.60
	IV	15	7.50	112.50
5 June	I	25	4.70	117.50
	IV	13	7.50	97.50
9 June	I	15	4.70	70.50
				717.00

Expenses

Date	Code	Description	$
1 June	85	Machine hire	400
			400

Production overheads

Hours	OAR	$

ACTIVITY 3

JOB COST CARD

Job number: 3867   Customer name: OT Ltd

Estimate ref: Quoted estimate:

Start date: 1 June   Delivery date: 17 June

Invoice number: 26457   Invoice amount: $7,800

COSTS:

Materials

Date	Code	Qty	Price	$
1 June	T73	40 kg	$60	2,400
5 June	R80	60 kg	$5	300
9 June	B45	280m	$8	2,240
				4,940

Labour

Date	Grade	Hours	Rate	$
1 June	II	43	5.80	249.40
2 June	II	12	5.80	69.60
	IV	15	7.50	112.50
5 June	I	25	4.70	117.50
	IV	13	7.50	97.50
9 June	I	15	4.70	70.50
				717.00

Expenses

Date	Code	Description	$
1 June	85	Machine hire	400
			400

Production overheads

Hours	OAR	$
123	4.00	492
		492

Cost summary:

Direct materials	4,940
Direct labour	717
Direct expenses	400
Production overheads	492
Administration overheads	156
Selling and distribution overheads	78
Total cost	6,783
Invoice price	7,800
Profit/loss	1,017

ACTIVITY 4

Answer **C**

Physical flow of units

	Units started		Units completed		Closing WIP
	350	=	275 (bal fig)	+	75

Equivalent units of production

Units started and finished	275
Closing WIP (75 × 60%)	45
	——
	320
	——

Cost per equivalent unit	=	$\dfrac{\$3,696}{320}$ =	£11.55
Value of finished goods	=	275 × £11.55 =	£3,176.00
Value of closing WIP	=	45 × £11.55 =	£520.00
			—————
			£3,696.00
			—————

ACTIVITY 5

Process account

	Units	£		Units	£
Material	1,000	70,000	Output	800	56,600
Labour		480	Work-in- progress	200	14,120
Overhead		240			
	———	———		———	———
	1,000	70,720		1,000	70,720
	———	———		———	———

Statement of equivalent units and statement of cost

Element of cost	Comp output	WIP	Equivalent units	Cost £	Cost per unit
Direct materials	800	200	1,000	70,000	70.00
Direct labour	800	160	960	480	0.50
Overhead	800	160	960	240	0.25
					———
					£70.75
					———

			£
Completed output	800 tonnes × £70.75		56,600
Work-in-progress			
Direct materials	200 tonnes × £70.00	14,000	
Direct labour	160 tonnes × £0.50	80	
Overhead	160 tonnes × £0.25	40	
			14,120

EXAM-STYLE QUESTIONS

1   D

$$2{,}400 \times \frac{100}{80} \times \$10 = \$30{,}000$$

2   C

Overheads are charged to jobs at predetermined absorption rate.

3   D

Statement A is correct. Job costs are identified with a particular job, whereas process costs (of units produced and work-in-process) are averages, based on equivalent units of production.

Statement B is also correct. Each repair job is likely to be different so job costing will be more suitable.

Statement C is correct, because without data about units completed and units still in process, losses and equivalent units of production cannot be calculated.

Statement D is incorrect, because the cost of normal loss will usually be incorporated into job costs as well as into process costs. In process costing this is commonly done by giving normal loss no cost, leaving costs to be shared between output, closing WIP and abnormal loss/gain. In job costing it can be done by adjusting direct materials costs to allow for normal wastage, and direct labour costs for normal reworking of items or normal spoilage.

4   B   **Process B – Account**

	Units	$		Units	$
Raw materials	13,500	60,750.00	Output	11,750	141,000.00
Overheads		16,875.00	Closing WIP	1,750	14,437.50
Labour		77,812.50			
	13,500	155,437.50		13,500	155,437.50

Closing WIP units	=	Input units – output units
	=	13,500 – 11,750
	=	1,750

Each uncompleted unit is valued at:

	$
Transferred materials	4.50
Overheads	1.25
Labour	2.50
	8.25

1,750 units × $8.25 = $14,437.50

5 **A**

	Total	*Material*	*Labour and o/h*
Finished goods	1,700	1,700	1,700
Closing inventory	300	150	90
	2,000	1,850	1,790
Cost		$5,550	$4,475
Cost per equivalent unit		$3	$2.50
Value of closing inventory	$675	$450	$225

Equivalent units

6 **A**

100 units that are 60% complete are 60 equivalent units.

CHAPTER 10

ACTIVITY 1

Actual output measured in standard hours = 1,100 ÷ 4

= 275 hours

Production volume ratio = $\dfrac{\text{Actual output measured in standard hours}}{\text{Budgeted production hours}} \times 100\%$

= $\dfrac{275}{300} \times 100\%$

= 91.67%

The actual production volume achieved during the period was 8.33% lower than budgeted. This could have been achieved either through working fewer hours than budgeted (the capacity utilisation ratio) or through working less efficiently than standard (the efficiency ratio). Looking at these ratios will reveal the causes.

Capacity utilisation ratio $= \dfrac{\text{Actual hours worked}}{\text{Budgeted hours}} \times 100\%$

$= \dfrac{250}{300} \times 100\%$

$= 83.33\%$

Just under seventeen per cent less capacity than budgeted was made available and utilised during the period.

Efficiency ratio $= \dfrac{\text{Actual output measured in standard hours}}{\text{Actual hours worked}} \times 100\%$

$= \dfrac{275}{250} \times 100\%$

$= 110\%$

Despite, or perhaps because of lower capacity, the workforce worked at a 110% efficiency level, which negated part of the losses made through lower capacity.

Check: 83.33% × 110% = 91.67%

ACTIVITY 2

		Division A	Division B
(a)	ROCE	$\dfrac{15,800}{106,700} \times 100\% = 14.8\%$	$\dfrac{27,300}{210,000} \times 100\% = 13.0\%$

(b)	Residual income				
		Profit	$15,800		$27,300
		Interest			
		($106,700 × 11%)	$11,737	($210,000 × 11%)	$23,100
		RI	$4,063		$4,200

(c)   Asset turnover

$\dfrac{160,050}{106,700} = 1.5$ $\dfrac{252,000}{210,000} = 1.2$

Division B earns a lower ROCE than division A, i.e. division B generates less profit per $1 invested in the division. Both divisions earn a return which is higher than the cost of capital, since both generate a positive residual income. Although division B earns a lower percentage return, the capital invested in the division is much greater and this results in a higher residual income for division B. The asset turnover for division A is 1.5 and for division B it is 1.2. This means that division A seems to make a higher return on the assets that it employs than division B does.

EXAM-STYLE QUESTIONS

1   **B**   The manager of a cost centre has no control over revenues therefore a performance measure based on profit would not be appropriate.

2   **B**   The ROCE is 185/1,540 × 100% = 12.0%

3

		True	False
(a)	A production volume ratio of 110% means that overall production is 10% higher than planned levels.	x	
(b)	A capacity utilisation ratio of 95% means that actual hours of production are 5% less than planned.	x	
(c)	An efficiency ratio of 105% means that 5% more units were produced than planned.		x

An efficiency ratio of 105% means that workers produced 5% more per hour for each hour worked but overall production levels depend on how many hours were actually worked compared to that expected (i.e. also the capacity utilisation ratio).

CHAPTER 11

ACTIVITY 1

Key advantages of computers:

*   speed of processing and communication/transmission

*   accuracy

*   volume (processing and storage)

*   cost-efficient compared with manual systems

*   user-friendly presentation with many standard software packages

*   accessibility, via the Internet/a business intranet, from any location

*   flexibility of working (e.g. telecommuting).

*   Computers can provide information and recommend options to management, but they cannot exercise judgement nor can they take the responsibility for decisions.

EXAM-STYLE QUESTIONS

1   **D**

A line graph is best used when trying to show how two variables (such as production units and total variable costs) are related.

2   **C**

See section 5.1 of the text for a full explanation of each term.

3   **B**

The other functions will help the user manage large amounts of data, but they will still show some unwanted data. The filter function will only display the data that the user chooses to view.

4   **D**

Production   = sales + closing inventory– opening inventory

Closing inventory for Feb = opening inventory for March, so

Feb Production   = Feb sales + opening inventory March – opening inventory Feb

= C3 + D4 – C4

5   **B**

The production volume ratio is calculated as:

$$\frac{\text{Actual output measured in standard hours}}{\text{Budgeted production hours}} \times 100\%$$

Standard hour	=	B2/B3
Actual output measured in standard hours	=	C2/standard hours
	=	C2/(B2/B3)
	=	C2×B3/B2
Production volume ratio	=	(C2×B3/B2)/B3
	=	C2/B2

\INDEX

KAPLAN PUBLISHING